STUDIES IN HADĪTH METHODOLOGY AND LITERATURE

STUDIES IN HADĪTH METHODOLOGY AND LITERATURE

Muhammad Mustafa Azami, M.A., Ph.D.

Professor of Science of Hadith
University of Riyadh
Riyadh, Saudi Arabia

American Trust Publications
721 Enterprise Drive
Oak Brook, IL 60523

First Printing 1977

Reprinted 2012

Library of Congress Catalog Card No. 77-90335
ISBN No. 0-89259-011-4

American Trust Publications
721 Enterprise Drive
Oak Brook, IL 60523

Phone: (630) 789-9191 Fax: (630) 789-9455

Printed in the United States of America

CONTENTS

Part I: ḥadīth Methodology

Part II: Ḥadīth Literature

INTRODUCTION

A tremendous amount of literature is available in Arabic on the methodology of *Ḥadīth* but our new generation whose majority does not know Arabic is unable to benefit from it. Even those who speak Arabic find it difficult to use these books due to the terminology used in them. Only a few books on science of *Ḥadīth* have been written in English and most of them seem to be meant to confuse the readers. The only one in English which can claim scholarly merit is one by Professor Zubair Siddiqi. I read it some 15 years ago, but it is out of print now and unavailable. Therefore, I have written *Studies in Ḥadīth Methodology and Literature* to fulfill the need of College students, as well as that of educated laymen. I have avoided unnecessary details, and technical language as far as possible. I hope its careful reading would eliminate most of the doubts which have been created, deliberately or out of ignorance, by Orientalists and others and would provide basic knowledge of the subject. However, it would be naive to think that after reading this book one would gain the capacity ot criticise the *Ḥadīth*.

The book has been divided into two parts. In part One, I deal with the subject of *Ḥadīth* Methodology. In Part Two, I discuss the literature, introducing the six principal books, as well as six others which had great significance and represent a stage in the compilation of *Ḥadīth* books. Those interested in the early recording of *ḥadīth* may go through my book *Studies in Early Ḥadīth Literature* while the problem of *isnād* has been discussed in my work *On Schacht's Origins of Mahammadan Jurisprudence*. Much valuable information on the criticism of *ḥadīth* may be found in the introduction to *kitāb al-Tamyīz* of Imām Muslim. Thus these early works have contributed to many chapters of the present work.

Two of my colleagues Dr. M.S. Al-'Awwa and Dr. Ja'far Shaikh Idrīs took the trouble to read the manuscript. I have benefited from their criticism and clarification. May Allah reward them for their help.

Thanks are also due to Dr. El-Tigāni Abugideiri on whose initiative and persistent demand the book was written. One should not fail to mention Mr. Abdur Rahman of WAMY who worked hard to type the draft from my poor handwriting.

Finally, I apologize to the readers for giving my consent to the publication of this book even though the words صلّى الله عليه وسلّم have not been printed after the name of the Prophet صلّى الله عليه وسلّم or after the words "the Prophet." I regret this omission but at the time of writing this introduction it was too late to fill in the words of the blessing. May Allah forgive me.

1st Rajab, 1397/1977

M.M. AZAMI
College of Education
University of Riyadh
Riyadh, Saudi Arabia

LIST OF ABBREVIATIONS

A.	Abū
A.D.	Abū Dāwūd, *Sunan*
A. Awana	Ab8u 'Awāna
b.	bin
BU	Al-Bukhārī, *Ṣaḥīḥ*
Dārimi	*sunan*
Hanbal	Ibn Ḥanbal, *Musnad*
I.M.	Ibn, Māja, *Sunan*
Mizān	Dhahabī, *Mizān al-L'tidāl*
MU	Muslim, *Ṣaḥīḥ*
NAS	Nasā'i, *Sunan*
Rāzī	See Ibn Abu Hātim al-Rāzī, *Al-Jarḥ wa al-Ta'dīl*
Tayālisī	Abu Dawūd Ṭayālisī, *Sunan*
Tawsat	Tabarānī, *al-Mu'jam al-Awsat*
Tir	Tirmidhī, *Sunan*
Takbir	Ṭarānī, *al-Mu'jam al-Kabīr*
Studies	A'zami, *Studies in Early Ḥadīth Literature*
Zaid	Zaid b. 'Ali, *Musnad*

TRANSLITERATION

The transliteration of Arabic words in this book is according to the system indicated in the Encyclopedia of Islam.

Part One: *ḥadīth* Methodology

CHAPTER I

ḤADĪTH, ITS MEANING, CONCEPT AND AUTHORITY

The Word '*ḥadīth*' and its Meaning

The Arabic word *ḥadīth* literally means communication, story, conversation: religious or secular, historical or recent.

Whenever used as an adjective it means new. It has been used in the Qur'ān 23 times. Here are a few examples:

Usage of the Word *ḥadīth* in the Qur'ān for:

a) Religious communication, message or the Qur'ān:
Almighty Allah says: ﴾الله نَزَّلَ أَحسَنَ ٱلحديثِ كِتَابَاً﴿
"Allah has revealed (time after time) the most beautiful *ḥadīth* (Message) in the form of a book."[1]

Almighty Allah says: ﴾فَذَرونى ومَن يُكَذِّب بهذا ٱلحديث﴿
"Then leave Me alone with such as reject this *ḥadīth*."[2] (meaning the Qur'ān).[3]

b) Story of a secular or general nature:
Almighty Allah says: ﴾وإذا رأيتَ ٱلذين يخوضون فى آياتنا فاعْرِض عنهم حتى
يخوضوا فى حديث غيره﴿
"And whenever you meet such as indulge in (blasphemous) talk about Our Message, turn thy back upon them until they begin *ḥadīth* (conversation) of some other things."[4]

---

1. The Qur'ān, az-Zumr, 23.
2. Ibid., al-Qalam, 44.
3. Ibn Kathīr, Tafsīr, vii, 91.
4. The Qur'ān, al-An'ām, 68.

c) Historical story:
Almighty Allah says: ﴿وهل أتاك حديث موسىٰ﴾
"Has the *ḥadīth* (story) of Mūsā reached thee?"[5]

d) Current story or conversation:
Almighty Allah says: ﴿وإذ أسرَّ آلنبى إلى بعض أزواجه حديثا﴾
"When the Prophet confined a *ḥadīth* (a secret) to one of his wives."[6]

We may conclude that this word has been used in the Qur'ān in the sense of story or communication or message, be it religious or secular, from a remote past or of the present time.

Usage of the Word *'ḥadīth'* in the Sayings of the Prophet

The word was used in the same sense by the Prophet as it has been used in the Qur'ān. Here are a few examples:

a) Religious communication:
The Prophet says:[7] «أحسن الحديث كتاب الله»
"The best *ḥadīth* is the book of Allah"
And the Prophet says: «غفر الله امرءاً سمع منا حديثاً فحفظه حتى يبلغه فرب مبلغ أحفظ له من سامع»
"Allah illumines a man who hears *ḥadīth* from me, preserves it carefully and passes it on to others ..."[8]

b) Secular or general conversation or tale:
The Prophet says: «من استمع إلى حديث قوم وهم له كارهون أو يفرون منه ، صب فى أذنه الأنك»
"One who tries to eavesdrop on the *ḥadīth* (conversation) of the people when they dislike his doing so and want to keep away from him, in the Hereafter hot copper would be poured in his ear."[9]

c) Historical story:
The Prophet says: «حدثوا عن بنى إسرائيل»
"You may transmit *ḥadīth* from *Banu Israil.*"[10]

d) Current story, secret or conversation:
The Prophet says: «إذا حدَّث الرجل الحديث ثم التفت فهى أمانة»

"If someone tells a *ḥadīth* (secret) then goes his way, his words become a trust."[11]

---

5. Ibid., *Tāhā*: 9.
6. Ibid., *al-Tahrīm*: 3.
7. Bukhārī, *Adāb*: 70.
8. Hanba, I:437.
9 Bukhārī, *Tab'īr*: 45.
10 Bukhārī, *Anbiyā'*: 50.
11 Tirmidhi, *Birr*: 39.

It is clear now, in the light of the above mentioned examples that the word *ḥadīth* has, in its meaning, the sense of story or communication.

In the early days of Islam the stories and communications of the Prophet (*ḥadīth*) dominated all other kinds of communications, so this word began to be used almost exclusively for the narration about or from the Prophet.[12]

The Term *Ḥadīth* and its Meaning According to *Muhaddithīn* and Jurists

According to *Muhaddithīn* it stands for 'what was transmitted on the authority of the Prophet, his deeds, sayings, tacit approval, or description of his *ṣifāt* (features) meaning his physical appearance. However, physical appearance of the Prophet is not included in the definition used by the jurists.[13]

Thus *ḥadīth* literature means the literature which consists of the narrations of the life of the Prophet and the things approved by him. However, the term was used sometimes in much broader sense to cover the narrations about the Companions and Successors as well.[14]

Sometimes some other words were also used in the same sense, such as *khabar* and *athar*. Most of the scholars used these three terms: *ḥadīth*, *khabar* and *athar* as synonymous. However, some scholars mostly of Khurasan region used to differentiate between *khabar* and *athar*. They used the *khabar* in the sense of *ḥadīth*, and the term *athar* restricted to the sayings and decisions of the Companions. However, there is another key word, though a little different from the term *ḥadīth* in the meaning, yet used mostly as synonymous, that is the term *sunnah*. Due to the importance of this term we shall discuss it in some detail.

The Word *Sunnah*, its Meaning and Different Usage

Sunnah, according to Arabic lexicographers means: 'a way, course, rule, mode, or manner, of acting or conduct of life·'[15]

In the Qur'ān, the word *sunnah* and its plural *sunan* have been used sixteen times. In all of these cases it is used in the sense of established course of rule, mode of life, and line of cconduct.[16]

---

12. See Zafar Ansārī, *Islamic Juristic terminology*, p.5
13. See Al-Jazā'irī, Taujih an-Nazar, p. 2.
14. Jurjānī, *Risāla*, 1. for detailed reference see, Al-Azami, *Studies*, 302.
15. Lane, iv 1438.
16. See Penrice, *Dictionery of the Koran*, p. 73.

In Arabic literature, especially in the early *Ḥadīth-Fiqh* books it has been used in different meanings, such as:

Sharī'a

Established non-compulsory religious practice without its being *fard* or *wājib* (compulsory).

That which is proved by means of *sunnah*, one of the four Sources of Law.[17]

Ṭarīqat ad-Dīn

Model behaviour of the Prophet.

According to Abul Baqa' the term *sunnah* is not restricted as such to the *sunnah* of the Prophet or of his companions. In Shāfi'ī however, the use of the term *sunnah* is restricted to the *sunnah* of the Prophet alone. According to Arabic lexicography, as we have seen, it means 'mode of life', etc. Therefore, when Almighty Allah ordered Muslims to obey the Prophet and to take his life as a good model and follow it, the expression '*sunnah* of the Prophet' came into use. The usage began in the life of the Prophet, and it was used by him.

Sometimes the Arabic definite article (*AL*) was affixed to the word *sunnah* to denote the *sunnah* of the Prophet, while the general use of the word continued, though decreasing day by day. At the end of the second century it began to be used almost exclusively in the legal books for the norms set by the Prophet or norms deduced from the Prophet's norm.

As *sunnah* means the mode of life, and the *sunnah* of the Prophet's means the mode of the life of the Prophet, and *ḥadīth* means the narration of the life of the Prophet, these two terms were used almost interchangeably, though there is a slight difference between them. For a *ḥadīt* may not contain any *sunnah* or a single *ḥadīth* may contain more than one *sunnah*. However, to avoid confusion, we shall use them as interchangeable as they have been used by early scholars as well as by the present ones.

If *ḥadīth* literature stands for the narration concerning the Prophet and sometimes his Companions, then what do the sciences of *ḥadīth* stand for? To err is human. In reporting, narrating, and recording the life and conduct of the Prophet some mistakes were committed even by the most sincere scholars, not to speak of some unscrupulous men who deliberately fabricated materials pretending to be concerned with the Prophet. Therefore, the science of *ḥadīth* was developed to evaluate every single statement ascribed to the Prophet.

---

17 Thānawī *Kashshāf* 703ff

Why was this painstaking task done? There have been many great rulers and leaders but nothing of this sort was developed to differentiate between correct and incorrect statements attributed to them. The answer to this question is the unique position of the *sunnah* of the Prophet, which demanded this care.

The Authority of the Prophet

The scholars are unanimous that the authority of the Qur'ān is binding on all Muslims. The authority of the Prophet comes next only to the Qur'ān. His authority is not derived through the community's acceptance of the Prophet as a person of authority. His authority is expressed through Divine will. Allah describes His Prophet's position in the following way:

The Prophet Muhammad and His Position According to the Qur'ān

a) *Expounder of the Qur'ān*
The Prophet is the expounder of the Qur'ān appointed by Allah. Al-mighty Allah says: ﴿وأنزلنا إليك ٱلذِّكر لتبيِّنَ للناس ما نُزِّلَ إليهم ولعلَّهم يتفكَّرون﴾

"We have revealed unto thee the Remembrance, (the Qur'ān). that you may explain to mankind that which has been revealed for them."[18]

The Qur'ān commands – if we may take *ṣalāt* (prayer) as an example – the establishment of *ṣalāt* (prayer) is in numerous verses, but the details for the method of praying are not prescribed. The Prophet's task was to demonstrate the forms of prayer practically as well as orally.

b) *Legislator*
Almighty Allah, speaking about the legislative power of the Prophet says:
﴿ويُحِلُّ لهم ٱلطَّيِّبات ويُحرِّم عليهم ٱلخبائث ويضع عنهم إصرَهُم وٱلأغلال ٱلتي كانت عليهم﴾
"He will make lawful for them all good things and prohibit for them only the foul, and will relieve them of their burden and the fetters which they used to wear."[19] In this verse we find that the legislative authority is bestowed upon the Prophet. So he acts as the society's law giver. The Prophet initiated certain things which were later mentioned by the Qur'ān as the standardized practices of the community, e.g. the practice of *Adhān* to which the Qur'ān refers only as the 'existing practice'.[20] This instance proves the legislative authority of the Prophet and that his deeds were sanctioned by Allah.

---

18. The Qur'ān, *an-Naḥl*, 44.
19. Ibid., *al-A'rāf*: 157.
20. See Ibid., *al-Jumu'a*: 9.

c) *Model behavior for Muslim Society*

The Qur'ān refers to the life pattern of the Prophet.

﴿لَقد كان لكم فى رسول الله أُسْوَة حسنة لمن كان يرجو الله واليوم آلآخر وذكر الله كثيرا﴾

"A noble model you have in Allah's Apostle, for all whose hope is in Allah, and in the Final Day, and who often remember Allah."[21]

If we consider the Prophet as the model for the community, then Muslims have to follow his example in every way, especially as they have been specifically commanded to do so by Allah. These three essentials combined in the person of the Prophet lead to the inevitable conclusion that Muslim Society must follow the Prophet in every walk of life. Almighty Allah did not leave the question open to debate. He explicitly ordered total obedience to the Prophet.

d) *Total obedience to the Prophet*

Almighty Allah says:[22] ﴿وما أرسلنا من رسول إلا ليُطاع بإذن الله﴾

"We sent no messenger save that he should be obeyed by Allah's leave."

He further says: ﴿قل أطيعوا الله وآلرسول فإن تولّوْا فإن الله لا يحب آلكافرين﴾

"Say, 'Obey Allah, and the Messenger.' But if they turn their backs, Allah loves not the unbelievers."[23]

And says: ﴿وأطيعوا الله وآلرسول لعلكم تُرحمون﴾

Obey Allah and the Messenger haply so you will find mercy."[24]

He further says: ﴿ياأيُّها آلذين آمنوا أطيعوا الله وأطيعوا آلرسول وأولى آلأمر منكم فإن تنازعتم فى شىء فردوه إلى الله وآلرسول إن كنْتم تؤمنون بالله وآليوم آلآخر ذلك خير وأحسن تأويلا﴾

"O believers, obey Allah, and obey the Messenger and those in authority among you. If you quarrel on anything, refer it to Allah and the Messenger, if you believe in Allah and the Last Day: that is better, and fairer in the issue."[25]

In the light of these verses it becomes clear that the commands of Allah as well as the proven commands of the Prophet are binding on a Muslim. He has to obey both of them equally. The Prophet's total life is a good example for all Muslims, and ought to be followed by them. A Muslim should not feel hesitant in carrying out the orders of the Prophet. Obedience here means full and not half-hearted submission.

21. Ibid., *al-Aḥzāb*: 21.
22. Ibid., *an-Nisā'*: 64.
23. Ibid., *āl-'Imrān*: 32.
24. Ibid., *āl-'Imrān*: 132.
25. Ibid., *an-Nisā': 59, there are so many references in the Qur'ān that the question does not really need any reference on this subject.*

Allah says:[26] ﴿فلا وربك لا يؤمنون حتى يحكموك فيما شجر بينهم ثم لا يجدوا فى أنفسهم حرجا مما قضيت ويسلموا تسليما﴾

"But no, by thy Lord! they will not believe till they make thee the judge regarding disagreement between them and find in themselves no resistance against the verdict, but accept in full submission."

Before concluding this discussion, it is necessary to quote one more verse from the Qur'ān. Allah says:[27]

﴿وما آتاكم آلرسول فخذوه وما نهاكم عنه فانتهوا واتقوا الله إن الله شديد آلعقاب﴾

"And whatsoever the Messenger gives you, take it. And whatsoever he forbids, abstain from it."

These are some of the many Qur'ānic verses which state the authority of the Prophet and emphasize the fact that his whole life, decisions, judgements and commands have binding authority and ought to be followed in all spheres of life by Muslim individuals and communities as well as by Muslim States.

It is obvious that this authority of the Prophet does not rest on acceptance by the community or on the opinion of certain lawyers or scholars or the founders of the law schools. This point has been made clear by the Qur'ān. For this reason, the Muslim community accepted the authority of the Prophet from the very day the mission of the Prophet began and has accepted all his verbal commands, his deeds, his tacit approval as the way of life, a binding factor and a model which ought to be followed.

All the activities of the Prophet, were covered by the *sunnah* or the *sunnah* of the Prophet, which was and still is, and will remain one of the main sources of Islamic law, second only to the Qur'ān.

Sunnah of the Prophet

As I have mentioned earlier, the term '*sunnah*' as such is not restricted to the '*sunnah*' of the Prophet.[28] Therefore we find this term sometimes used for others than the Prophet as well, which resulted in some misunderstanding by modern scholars. It is claimed by some modern scholars that Shafi'i was the first to define *sunnah* as the model behavior of the Prophet. The problem would not have arisen if they had realized that the concept of *sunnah* predated the definition of that term.

---

26. Ibid., *an-Nisā': 65.*

27. *Ibid., al-Hashr*: 7. This verse was sent down in the context of the booty of war but it applies to all the cases as the Prophet explained. See Hanabal, i:415. Ibn Kathīr, *Tafsīr*, vi:604. Therefore it would be erroneous to confine it to the case of booty only. This is the general trend of the Qur'ān, a verse came for a certain occasion but it has general application.

28. For detailed study, see, A'zamī, *On Schacht's Origins of Muhammadan Jurisprudence*.

The powers of legislation, for example, are determined by the constitutions of modern states. When constitutions endorse the legislative powers and the range of their legislation, nobody can challenge them or claim rightfully that he is not to be bound by them. Thus – according to Islamic concepts – it is not for the lawyers but for Almighty Allah who is the Law-Giver to determine the legislative authority if there is any.

The Qur'ān never says that the source of law is *sunnah* so that the early time of obedience to the Messenger of Allah, which is obligatory, and mentions his example which ought to be followed. Therefore, even if one agrees that the early scholars used this word or term in a broad sense, it should not create any perplexity because the source of law is not this particular 'word' or 'term' but the concept which derives its authority directly from the Qur'ān.

When we come to this concept, we find it is clearly endorsed by the Qur'ān, as we have seen earlier, and explicitly accepted by early lawyers. Hence we may conclude that the *sunnah* of the Prophet is a must for Muslims, be they individuals, communities or states.

The *aḥādīth* of the Prophet are repositories for the *sunnah* of the Prophet, and therefore he must have made arrangements for its diffusion in the Muslim community. We shall discuss this point in the next chapter.

CHAPTER II

THE PROPHET AND HIS *AḤĀDĪTH* TEACHING, LEARNING AND DIFFUSION

Transmission of the *Ḥadīth* of the Prophet

The *ḥadīth,* the storeroom of the Prophet's *sunna* served an essential need of the Muslims, be they individuals or communities. In this chapter we shall try to sketch related activities and describe the means which were used to teach *aḥādīth* and to learn and preserve them, and the factors which helped the Companions in their task.

Teaching of the *Aḥādīth* by the Prophet

The methods used by the Prophet to teach his *sunna* or *hadīth* may be put in three categories:

1. Verbal teaching
2. Written medium (Dictation to scribes)
3. Practical demonstration.

1. *Teaching of sunna by the Prophet in verbal form*

The Prophet himself was the teacher of his *sunna*[1]. To make memorizing and understanding easy he used to repeat important things thrice[2]. After teaching the Companions he used to listen to what they had learnt[3]. Deputations arriving from outlying areas were given in charge of Madinites, not only to be accommodated but also for education in the Qur'ān and the *sunna.* The Prophet asked them questions to discover the extent of their learning[4].

2. *Teaching of sunna by the Prophet by written method*

All the letters of the Prophet to kings, rulers, chieftains, and Muslim governors can be included in the teaching of the *sunna* by written media.

---

1. See Al-Khaṭīb, *Al-Faqīh* ii, 124.
2. BU, *'Ilm,* 30.
3. BU, *Wuḍu',* 75.
4. See, Hanbal iv, 206.

Some of those letters are very lengthy and contain legal matters concerning *Zakāt,* taxation, forms of worship, etc.[5] We can estimate the numbers of letters which were probably sent by the Prophet and the recording activities related to them if we remember that he had at least 45 scribes who wrote for him at sometime or the other[6]. In the same category, we may put what was dictated by the Prophet to different Companions, such as 'Alī b. Abū Ṭalīb, and some of the writings of 'Abdullah b. 'Amr b. Āl-'Aṣ, and the Prophet's orders for delivering a copy of his *Khuṭba* to Abū Shāh, a Yaminite[7].

3. *Teaching of sunna by the Prophet by practical demonstration*

As far as practical demonstration is concerned, the Prophet taught the method of ablution, prayers, fasting and pilgrimage etc. In every walk of life, the Prophet gave practical lessons in excellence, with clear instructions to follow his practice. He said, 'pray as you see me praying[8]. He further said, 'learn from me the rituals of pilgrimage'[9].

In answer to many questions, he used to tell the questioner to stay with him and learn by observing his practice[10].

Measures Taken by the Prophet for the Diffusion of *Sunna*

1. *Establishment of Schools*

'Schools' were established by the Prophet in Madina very soon after his arrival[11]. His general policy was to send teachers and preachers to different areas outside Madina.

For Example delegates were sent to 'Adhal and Qāra in 3 A.H., to Bīr Ma'ūna in 4 A.H., to Najrān and to Yeman and Hadramaut in 9 A.H.[12].

2. *The Prophet's Directions about Diffusion of Knowledge*

The Prophet says: "Pass on knowledge from me even if it is only one verse"[13].

The same emphasis is noticeable in his oration at the farewell *Hajj* where the Prophet said: "Those who are present (here) should convey the

5. See Ḥamīdulla, *al-Wathā'iq al-Siyāsiyah.*
6. Al-Azami, *Kuttāb al Nabī,* 25-112.
7. BU. *'Ilm,* 39.
8. BU. *Adhān,* 18.
9. MU. *Ḥajj,* 310.
10. See for example, MU. *Masājid,* 176.
11. See for detail, al Azamī, *Studies in Early Ḥadīth literature,* p. 3-4.
12. See for detail, Azami, *Studies,* p. 4-5.
13. BU. *Anbiyā',* 50.

message to those who are absent.[14]. It was therefore, a common practice among Companions to tell absentees about the Prophet's deeds and sayings. Delegations coming to Madina were ordered to teach their people after returning. For instance, Mālik b. Al-Huwairith was ordered by the Prophet, at his departure, to teach the people, a duty which he carried on even long after the death of the Prophet[15]. The same kind of direction was given to other delegations as well.[16] When the delegation of 'Abdul Qaīs came to the Prophet, it asked the Prophet that they should be taught so that they may convey teachings from the Prophet and teach their followers[17].

3. *Creation of incentive for teachers and students*

The Prophet not only gave directions to educate the people but also mentioned great rewards for teachers and students.

He stated that learning and the pursuit of knowledge is obligatory on every Muslim.[18] One who conceals knowledge is liable to go to hell[19], a fact which is mentioned in the Qur'ān.[20]

(a) *Rewards for students:*

The Prophet said: "If any one pursues a path in search of knowledge Allah will thereby make easy for him a path to paradise, and the angels spread their wings from good pleasure with one who seeks knowledge, and all the inhabitants of the heavens and the earth, even fish in the depths of water, ask forgiveness for him."[21]

(b) *Rewards for teachers:*

In this regard, the Prophet said: "When a man dies, his acts come to an end, with three exceptions: *Sadaqa Jārīya* (recurring charity), knowledge from which benefit continues to be reaped, and the prayers of a good son for him."[22]

(c) *Threat of Punishment:*

For those who refuse to be tempted into the educative process even by

---

14. BU. *'Ilm*, 9.
15. See Ibn Sa'd, vii, I, 29-30.
16. BU. *'Ilm*, 25.
17. BU. *Manāqib*, 5.
18. Ibn Māja, *Sunan*, Intr. 17.
19. Hanbal, II, 263.
20. The Qur'ān, II, 159, 174.
21. Hanbal, V, 196.
22. MU. *Waṣiya*, 14. It means both male and female.

these rewards, the Prophet seems to have indicated punishment which would inevitably come as a result of not teaching and not learning.[23]

I have now stated how the Prophet taught his *sunna* to the Muslim community and the measures he took to spread it and to make the people active in its pursuit and what sort of rewards and punishment were mentioned. Let us see what was the response of the community to all these, and how the *sunna* of the Prophet was received by the Companions.

How the *Sunna* of the Prophet was Received by the Companions

Some of the measures taken by the Prophet for the diffusion of *sunna* have been mentioned. Now we shall see what methods were applied by the recipients and what were the factors which helped them to learn those *sunna*.

It ought to be remembered that people always try to watch and thus remember the sayings and deeds of their beloved one. In this regard one can say with certainty that Muhammad was the most beloved person on earth in his community, and no one can stand beside him in this regard in the long history of humanity. Here I am going to quote a statement of one of his Companions to one of his deadly foes at that time.

> Safwān b. Umayya bought Zayd (the Companion of the Prophet who was betrayed and taken prisoner by polytheists) to kill him in revenge for his father Ummaya by Khalaf. Ṣafwān sent him with a freedman of his called Nistās to al-Tan'īm and they brought him out of the *Ḥaram* to kill him. A number of Quraysh gathered, among whom was Abū Sufyan b. Harb, who said to Zayd as he was brought out to be killed, "I adjure you by Allah, Zayd, don't you wish that Muhammad was with us now in your place so that we might cut off his head, and that you were with your family?" Zayd answered, "By Allah, I don't wish that Muhammad be in my place now or that even a thorn should hurt him or I were sitting with my family." Abu Sufyān used to say, 'I have never seen a man who was so loved as Muhammad's Companions loved him; Nisṭās killed him (Zayd), Allah have mercy upon him."[24]

---

23. al-Haithamī, *Majma' al-Zawā'id*, i, 164. This *ḥadīth* has a dubious *isnād* and is not well authenticated.
24. *Ibn Isḥāq, Sirat Rasūlullah*, translated by A. Guillume, p. 427-8, However I have used the word Allah for God, not as it was translated, as well as changed the translation in some places.

Thus the Prophet was the most beloved one in his community. The community's involvement in worldly pursuits was still minimal and thus a wider scope and greater opportunity for learning was available. Moreover, the Arabs had excellent memories. They used to remember by heart many verses of their tribal poets and others. When we recollect all these factors, as well as methods applied by the Prophet to teach his *sunna,* it becomes clear that its learning was very easy for the Muslim community. However, they were not content with these natural facilities but utilized every possible method for its learning and preservation.

Companions Learning of the *Aḥādīth*

The Companions used all the three methods of learning: (a) memorization (b) recording (c) through practise, following the method applied by the Prophet for teaching the *sunna.*

(a) *Learning by memorizing:*

The Companions used to listen to every word of the Prophet with utmost care. They used to learn the Qur'ān and the *ḥadīth* from the Prophet mostly in the mosque. When the Prophet went away for any reason, they started to recollect what they had learned. This practice has been described very well by Mu'āwīya[25]. The same evidence can be seen in the statement of Abū al-Dardā'.[26] This practice can be seen in its culmination in the statement of Anas b. Mālik, the servant of the Prophet. He says, "We sat with the Prophet, maybe sixty persons in number and the Prophet taught them *ḥadīth.* Later on when he went out for any necessity, we used to memorize it amongst us, when we departed it was as if cultivated in our hearts."[27]

The Companions faced the problems of daily life and its requirements as does everybody. So it was not practically possible for all of them to attend the circle of the Prophet on every occasion. Therefore, those who were absent sometimes from the educational circle of the Prophet used to learn from those who were present. This process has been described very well by the Companion Barā' b. 'Āzib[28]. Some of them came to an agreement between themselves to attend the circle of the Prophet in shifts, as we find in the case of 'Umar[29].

---

25. al-Ḥākim, *al-Mustadrak,* i, 94.
26. Ibn Ḥanbal, Musnad, vi, 443.
27. Khatīb, *al-Jāmi',* 43a.
28. Ibn Ḥanbal, *'Ilal,* 96b; al-Hākim, *al-Mustadarak,* 1, 127.
29. Ibn Sa'd, VIII, 136, BU. *'Ilm,* 27.

This practice reached its highest point in the case of the Companion Sulait. A piece of land was given to him by the Prophet. He used to stay there for some time and then return to Madina to learn what had been taught in his absence. The Companions used to inform him about the newly revealed portions of the Qur'ān and the judgment of the Prophet in different cases. He was so embarrassed that he requested the Prophet that the land should be taken back from him as it stopped him from the attendance in the Prophet's circle.[30]

This was the atmosphere and environment in which the teaching and learning of *ḥadīth* was carried on.

(b) *Companions' learning of aḥādīth through writing:*

The Companions learned the *ahādīth* by recording it in writing as well. There were good numbers of Companions who recorded the *aḥādīth* of the Prophet.[31]

(c) *Companions' learning of aḥādīth by practice*

It is essential to remember that the Companions put into practice whatever they learned by heart or by writing. The knowledge in Islam is for practice, not knowledge for the sake of knowledge, and the Companions knew this well. It is sufficient to note that Ibn 'Umar took eight years to learn the second *sura* of the Qur'ān[32].

This is a sketch of how the *ḥadīth* was learned by the Companions in the lifetime of the Prophet. After his death, the pattern remained almost the same except that the Messenger of Allah was no more among them. Now we shall throw some light on the subject in the period after the Prophet's death.

Learning of *Aḥādīth* in the Period of the Companions

Recollection of *Aḥādīth*

Recollection of *aḥādīth* was carried out in the time of the Companions as it was in the days of the Prophet. Abū Hurairah used to divide the night in three portions; one third for sleeping, one third for prayer and one third for the recollection of the *ḥadīth* of the Prophet.

'Umar and Abū Mūsā al-Ash'arī memorized *ḥadīth* through the night till the morning. We find the same in the case of Ibn 'Abbās and Zaid b. Arqam. Ibn Buraidah reports a similar situation with Mu'āwīya in the Syrian city of Ḥims.

30. Abū 'Ubaid, *al-Amwāl,* p. 272-3.
31. For detail see al-Azami, *Studies* 34-80.
32 Suyuṭī, *Durr al-Manthūr,* I, 21 quoting *Muw.* of Mālik.

On the other hand, we find a good number of the Companions such as 'Ali b. Abu Tālīb, Ibn Mas'ūd, Ibn 'Abbās, and Abū Sa'īd al-Khudrī advising the Successors on the memorizing of *ḥadīth*. So the same pattern of learning of *ḥadīth* continued in the time of the successors. They used to memorize *aḥādīth* either in groups or individually[1].

Official Patronage for the Teaching of the Qur'an and the *Sunna* of the Prophet

'Umar, the second Caliph, entrusted his governors with the duty of teaching the Qur'ān and the *sunna* of the Prophet[2]. He used to send teachers for this purpose in good numbers. He even sent a teacher to beduoins to find out the extent of their knowlẹdge of the Qur'ān[3].

Non-Official Activities

All the Companions who had knowledge of *ḥadīth* of the Prophet took part in its diffusion whenever they had the opportunity or felt the necessity. However, they may be put into two groups.

Those who used to impart knowledge when they thought that the people were in need of it. They felt compelled to teach because they knew very well the sin of hiding the knowledge.

Those who gave much time for this purpose and used to teach regularly.

At this point we need to pay attention to some new factors. After the Prophet's death his Companions took up his mission. A quarter of a century after the death of the Prophet, Islam spread to Afghanistan, a part of what is now the U.S.S.R., Iran, Syria, Iraq, Egypt, and Libya. The Companions of the Prophet were pioneers in this activity which implies that knowledge of the *aḥādīth* of the Prophet went with those Companions throughout the Muslim world. It also implies that not all the knowledge of *sunna* remained in Madina. Probably a certain *sunna* was known to a particular Companion, who went to Iraq or Egypt or somewhere else. Before the Companions died they entrusted the torch of *ahādīth* knowledge to the next generation which had to learn and be ready to take the responsibility. However, some unique conditions had been laid down for learning by *muhaddithin* and these are discussed in the next chapter.

---

1. For detail see, Al-Azami, *Studies*, 184.
2. Ibn Sa'd, III, I, 201; 243; Ibn Ḥanbal, *Musnad*, I, 48.
3. Ibn Ḥajar, *al-Iṣābah*, 'Auṣ b. Khālid al-Tā'ī, No. 332.

CHAPTER III

TAḤAMMUL AL-'ILM
CARRYING OF KNOWLEDGE OF *AḤĀDĪTH*

We have seen earlier how the Prophet taught his *aḥādīth* and *sunna* and how it was received by the Companions. As the Companions were direct disciples of the Prophet, they had the special privilege and duty to spread his teachings. However in later days, as the knowledge of *aḥādīth* spread all over the Muslim world, gathering of knowledge or collection of *ḥadīth* required much more extensive travelling, so new methods of learning had to be developed. These will be discussed here briefly.

Learning of *Aḥādīth* in Early Days

For learning of *ḥadīth* the following eight methods were in use:

(1) *Samā':* that is reading by the teacher to the students.

(2) *'Arḍ:* reading by students to teachers.

(3) *Ijāzah:* to permit someone to transmit a *ḥadīth* or book on the authority of the scholar without reading by any one.

(4) *Munāwalah:* to hand someone the written material to transmit.

(5) *Kitābah:* to write *aḥādīth* for someone.

(6) *I'lām:* to inform someone that informer has permission to transmit certain material.

(7) *Waṣīyah:* to entrust someone his books.

(8) *Wajādah:* to find some books or *aḥādīth* written by someone just as we nowadays discover some manuscripts in a library or somewhere else.

But in the period of the Companions only the first of these methods was in general use, while the use of other methods was negligible. The students stayed near their teachers at all times serving them and learning from them. When they imparted any *ḥadīth* the students wrote it down or memorized it. Al-Zuhrī says: "People used to sit with Ibn 'Umar, but none dared ask him questions till someone came from outside and asked him. We sat with Ibn al-Musayyab without questioning him, till someone came and questioned him. The question roused him to impart *ḥadīth* to us, or he began to impart it at his own will."[1] A little later the most common methods were numbers one and two. There has been a lot of discussion as to whether the first or the second is the best method of learning. In view of some scholars both methods have equal merit and Ṭaḥāwī (d. 328) wrote a booklet on the subject giving his opinion for the equality of both methods. Different terminology was used in transmitting the *ḥadīth* to show what method was used in learning the *ḥadīth*, as we see later. A man was not entitled to use any *ḥadīth* in his literary life if he had not received it by one of the eight above mentioned ways, that is up to number seven. Number eight was not recognized by the scholars. Now we shall discuss these methods in some detail.

(1) *Samā'*: سمـــــــاع Reading by the Teacher to Students

This method has the following features:

Oral recitation, reading from books, questions and answers, and dictation.

Oral Recitation of Aḥādīth by the Teacher

This practice began to decline from the second half of the second century, though it persisted to a much lesser extent for a long period. Usually, the students were attached to a certain teacher for a very long time, until they were believed to be authorities on the *aḥādīth* of their teachers. Sometimes they were called *Rāwī* or *Ṣāḥib* of so and so. Even if regular meetings were held for the teaching, only a few *aḥādīth* were taught in one lesson, say about three or four.

Reading from Books

Reading by the teacher, from his own book, which was preferred.

Reading by the teacher from the student's book, which was either a copy of or a selection from his own work. This method had a great many pitfalls for the teachers who did not learn their *aḥādīth* by heart. Some students and scholars played tricks. They would insert *aḥādīth* here and there into the teacher's *aḥādīth* and hand the book to the teacher for reading, to examine the soundness of his knowledge and memory. Teachers who failed to recognize the additional material were denounced and declared untrustworthy.

1. *Studies* 284.

Questions and Answers

In this method students used to read a part of the *ahādīth* and the teacher read it in full.

Dictating the Aḥādīth

Apart from the Prophet's dictation and his Companions' rare dictations of *aḥādīth,* perhaps the Companion Wāthilah b. Asqa' (d.83) was the first who held classes for dictation. This method was not encouraged in the early days because in this way a student could gather much knowledge in a very short time without much effort. It seems that al-Zuhrī was the first to depart from this attitude. About the end of the first century we find him dictating *aḥādīth,* a method which he followed during the rest of his life.

There were certain scholars who had an extreme distaste for dictation and did not allow writing down. There were others who did not transmit *aḥādīth* until the students wrote them down. Some of them even refused to dictate *aḥādīth* if the students used wooden boards from which the writing could be erased. There were some others who wrote down *aḥādīth* and after memorizing erased them. Others used to learn by heart and after memorizing wrote them down. It seems that compared with other methods of the teaching of *aḥādīth,* these were rare and uncommon practices. From the second century onwards, besides the usual method of reading from books, dictations became usual. Sometimes regular classes were held for this purpose.

The Method of Dictation For dictation, two methods were employed: either from a book or from memory. In some cases the students refused to write *aḥādīth* being dictated from memory, yet it seems that it was the fashion of the time to rely on memory in transmitting or dictating *aḥādīth.* Perhaps it was a matter of prestige and reputation. This practice resulted in many mistakes owing to the inherent deficiencies of memory. The teachers had to go through their books to refresh their memories. In many cases when they were uncertain they did not dictate.

The Mustamlīs The dictation method, due to large audience, gave rise to a new type of work for certain people who were called *Mustamlīs.* They used to repeat the words of the *Shaikh* in a loud voice to the audience.

To Select Someone for Writing As all the students could not write rapidly, sometimes a fast writer was chosen to take down *aḥādīth,* while others watched him writing, lest he should make any mistake. Later, either they borrowed the books or copied them in the presence of the owner. In literary circles a class of scribes or *Warrāqun* was found for the purpose of copying, which gave rise to trade in books.

The Correction of Written Copies It seems that the scholars were aware of the importance of revision after copying. Therefore we find them constantly advising their students, even helping them, in revision after copying. We find this practice from a very early stage. 'Urwah (22-93 H.) asked his son Hishām whether or not he revised after copying. Hishām replied, No, upon which 'Urawah said that in fact it meant he did not write down[2].

After copying or dictating, either the students helped each other to correct the copies or did so under the supervision of their masters.

The Writing Materials It seems that wooden boards were mostly used for writing dictations and taking notes from which, later on, fair copies were made. A special shorthand method was sometimes used to save time and space.

(2) *'Arḍ*: عــــــــــرض Reading to Teachers

Another method was that the book was read by the students to the teacher or by a certain man called a 'Qārī', and other students compared *aḥādīth* with their books or only listened attentively. Later they copied from the books. This method was called *'arḍ*. Unfamiliarity with this terminology may cause misunderstanding even to Arabs.

It seems that *'arḍ* was the most common practice from the beginning of the second century. In this case either copies were provided by the teachers themselves as many of them had their own scribes, *Kātib* or *Warrāq*, or students had their own books, copied earlier either from the original or from another copy of the same work. In copying they usually made a circular mark after every *ḥadīth*[3]. Whenever a student finished the reading of a *ḥadīth* he made a sign in the circle or somewhere else to show that this *ḥadīth* had been read to the teacher. This was necessary because even when a student knew *aḥādīth* through books he was not entitled to use those materials for teaching or for his own compilation till he received them through properly recognized methods of learning. If one did not follow this method, he could be accused of stealing ḥadīth, *'sāriq al-ḥadīth'*, which meant that a scholar used materials in teaching or in compiling his book which, even though genuine, were not obtained through the proper way. A modern parallel to this practice is the copyright law. A man can buy a million copies of a book but may not print even a few copies without per-

2. Khaṭīb Baghdādī, *Kifāyah*, 237.
3. See for detail, see Azami, *Studies*.

mission. The early scholars had their own method of copyright, where one could not use materials simply by buying a book[4].

When a *ḥadīth* was read more than once the students made additional marks for every reading. Sometimes scholars read the same book several times.

(3) *Ijāzah*: اجـــــــازة Permission

In *ḥadīth* terminology *Ijāzah* means to permit someone to transmit a *hadīth* or a book on the authority of a certain scholar who gave this permission, without having read the book to him. There have been different kinds of *Ijāzah*. Until the third century, it is difficult to find signs of the *Ijāzah* system, but it was widely used later. There have been differences of opinions about its validity.

This system, in certain cases, provided a kind of safeguard for the text. For example when A permitted B to transmit *Ṣaḥīḥ* of Bukhārī through the authority of A, then B ought to find out a copy of *Ṣaḥīḥ* of Bukhārī which contained a reading certificate including the name of A. In this way the correct text could be kept free of alterations.

(4) *Munāwala*: مناولـــــــة Handing the Book to a Student

When someone gave a student a manuscript along with the authority to transmit it. For example Zuhrī (51-124) gave his manuscripts to several scholars, like Thaurī, Auzā'ī and 'Ubaidullah b. 'Umar[5]. It was called *munāwala*. This was not a common practice in the early days.

(5) *Kitābah*: كتابـــــــة Correspondence

This means writing *aḥādīth* to give them to someone else to transmit. In modern terminology this could be called learning by correspondence. There were quite a good deal of activities of this sort. This practice started from very early days, and can be assumed to have started from the very beginning. Official letters of the rightly guided Caliphs contained many *aḥādīth* which were transmitted by scholars. Besides this many companions and later on many many scholars wrote down *aḥādīth* and sent them to

---

4. However, some scholars copied information from certain manuscripts which they found and explained it explicitly that they had found so and so in certain manuscript. This had no validity in the view of early scholars, because a copy might be forged one or the scribe might have committed mistakes in its reading.
5. See for detail, Azami, *Studies*, p. 88-93.

their students. See for example Ibn 'Abbās's writings to Ibn Abū Mulaikah and Najdah[6].

(6) *I'lām:* اعلام To Inform About *Aḥadith*

I'lām meant to inform someone that informer has permission to transmit a certain book on certain scholars' authority. Some of the scholars permitted this method of transmitting *aḥādīth* while others rejected it. The only benefit from it was that the second person had to find the original copy which bore the certificate and the name of the person who gave permission. Signs of this method are difficult to trace in the early period.

(7) *Wasīyah* وصية

To entrust someone the book which may be transmitted on the authority of the one who entrusted the books. For example Abū Qilābah (d. 104) who entrusted his books to Ayyūb al-Sakhtiyānī[7].

(8) *Wajadah* وجد

That is to find someone's book without any sort of permission to transmit on anyone's authority. This was not a recognized way of learning *aḥādīth*. According to the standard of the *Muḥaddithīn* one must state explicitly that the information he presented had been taken from the book of such a man. There are references to books of this sort from very early days. An example is the book of Sa'd b. 'Ubādah (d. 15 A.H.).[8]

Terms Used to Describe Transmission of *Aḥadith:*

There are many terms employed by *muḥaddithīn* for this purpose. As every *isnād* contains many names therefore these terms are repeated frequently.

To save space and time *Muḥaddithīn* used abbreviations or, say, shorthand method for this purpose, and even used to drop some word from *isnād*. These are the terms:

Haddathanā; حدثنا mostly written ثنا *Thanā* or *Nā* نا only.

Akhbaranā: أخبرنا mostly written أنا *Ana* only and rarely أرنا *arana*

Ḥaddathanā is used mostly to denote learning through the reading by the teacher (1st method)

6. For details see, Azami, *Studies* P. 41-2.
7. For details see, Azami, *Studies,* 63.
8. For detail see, Azami, *Studies,* 63.

Akhbaranā: is used to denote learning through the second method, though some of the scholars used these two terms interchangeably.

Anb'anā أنبأنا is used in *Ijāzah* and *munāwala,* and sometimes even *Ḥaddathanā Ijāzatan,* is used in *Munāwala.*

Sami'ah: سمع it is used in the learning through the first method only.

'An: عن it can be used in all the methods.

All these terms are not of equal value. *Sami'tu, Ḥaddathanā, Ḥaddathanī, Akhbaranā and Akhbaranī* are the most superior, though the authorities differ about which is best among them. However, *'an* is very inferior.

These terms should not be changed in copying. *'An* is not explicit for direct contact between narrators, therefore in case of a narrator who was accused of practising *Tadlīs,*[9] it might cause the *ḥadīth* to be judged a weak one.

Certificate of Reading

A regular record of attendance was kept and after the reading of a book was completed, a note was written either by the teacher or one of the famous scholars in attendance. This gave details of the attendance, e.g. who listened to the complete book and who joined partially, what part they read and what part was missed by them, giving dates and the places. If an attendant was under five years his age was mentioned with the title حضر which meant "attended." If he was five or more he was mentioned as a regular student. At its conclusion the book was usually signed by the teacher or by some famous attending scholar. In many cases, this certificate stipulated that no further entry could be made in the book which had been completed.[10]. This certificate was called *Ṭabāq* by the *Muḥaddithīn.*

Education in *ḥadīth* was free. Only a few scholars charged some money but they were denounced for this practice. The students' relations with their teachers were based on reverence and respect. Some of them used to help or serve their tutors, but there were tutors who did not accept any kind of service lest it might be taken as service in return for teaching.

In many cases, the teachers even helped their students financially, and it was quite common to offer meals to them. A noteworthy phenomenon of the education in *ḥadīth* was the continuous traveling of students and scholars to collect *aḥādīth.* Perhaps journeying was an essential part of studentship. Al-Khaṭīb al-Baghdādī wrote a book on the subject[11].

---

9. See for example Ibn Wahb, *Jāmi',* p. 40, 77.
10. For explanation of *Tadlīs,* see below, p. 65
11. See Khatīb, *ar-Riḥla*

The Ages of Students

First they learned the Qur'ān, mostly by heart. Many scholars used to examine new students in the Qur'ān. They also learned some other subjects such as Islamic Law, religious practices and grammar. Usually, they joined *Muhaddithīn's* circle around the age of twenty. In the era of the Successors students were about twenty years of age when they started learning *ahādīth*[12].

Zuhrī spoke of Ibn 'Uyayanah who was fifteen years old as the youngest student he had ever seen. Mūsā b. Isḥāq says the Kufans sent their sons to learn *aḥādīth* when they were twenty. Al-Thaurī and Abū al-Ahwaṣ, give 20 years as the age at which study of *ḥadīth* began. The Syrians began to write at 30. The Basrites began to learn when they were only 10; Ibn Ḥanbal started when he was 16. It ought to be remembered that this was a common practice in literary circles, with many exceptions, and not a compulsory rule which must be followed by everybody. However in later periods it was not observed. Al-Dabarī transmitted 'Abd al-Razzāq's book, and when 'Abd al-Razzāq died his student was not more than 7 years old[13]. It was said that if a child could discriminate between a cow and a donkey then he could start learning *aḥādīth*[14]. It was at the time when the texts had been fixed, and learning meant transmission of a book through channels of *Isnād.* On the other hand, especially in the second century, many scholars were considered weak in their *aḥādīth* from certain teachers on the grounds of their youth when they wrote down from them. For example, 'Amr al-Bairuti is considered weak in the *aḥādīth* of Auzā'ī as he was young when he wrote down from Auzā'ī. Similar charges were made against Ibn al-Madīnī, Ibn Abū Shaibah, Hishām b. Hassān etc.

However, later the situation changed completely. People began to bring even their infants to the lectures on *ḥadīth*. The attendance of a child at such lectures entitled him to a certificate which gave the name of the child, if he was under five, as proof that he attended the lectures. But if a child was five or more it was mentioned in the certificate (*Ṭibāq*) that he learned certain books from certain scholars.

This practice, according to which a child of five years was awarded a certificate of matriculation or graduation in *ḥadīth* sounds like a joke. But as a matter of fact the case is not so ridiculous as it seems and the practice was not as silly as it appears to be.

12. See Rāmhurmuzī, *Al-Muḥaddith*, 186.
13. Khatīb, *Kifāyah*, 64.
14. *Ibid.*, 65.

Let us see what was the task of this 'graduate' of 5 years in *ḥadīth* when he grew up. All he had to do was to *read* the text. Usually he was not supposed to interpret or explain it so his learning would not have much effect on its explanation.

The main use of this certificate was to mark the purity and authenticity of the text itself. The graduate's name was put in the certificate of reading which was not written on a sheet of paper but either on the margin of the book, or at the title or at the end of the book[15]. After being grown up, he was not entitled to read any copy of the same book. No, he must read either from the same manuscript or from a copy transcribed from the book which bore his name and which was checked carefully.

Therefore, by this very means, the scholars were able to safeguard the purity of the text while keeping the *isnād 'Alī,* that is the least number of scholars between the reader and the Prophet.

The Number of Students

There are references to hundreds of teachers from whom al-Thauri, Ibn al-Mubārak, al-Zuhrī, etc. had written down *aḥādīth.* In the works of biographers we find a long list of teachers and students of eminent scholars. For example, even if we take only one scholar, al-Zuhrī, we do not know precisely how many students wrote down from him, and how many attended his lectures. However, we have at least fifty references to his students who made their written collections from him.[16] The growing number of transmitters resulted in tremendous growth in the number of books. The books grew so voluminous that it was difficult to handle them. Therefore, to avoid chaos and discrepancies, Shu'bah advised writing the famous *aḥādīth* from the famous scholars.

This growth of books resulted in the growth of numbers of *aḥādīth.* A contributing factor was the method of *Muḥaddithīn* who counted every *isnād* as one *ḥadīth.* Thus if a single statement of the Prophet is narrated by one hundred *isnāds* it would be counted as one hundred *ḥadīth.* Thus a few thousand *aḥādīth* of the Prophet reached to over 600,000 *aḥādīth.* This fact and method which is unknown to many modern scholars caused them to make many mistakes.[17]

---

15. See Appendix No. 1.
16. For detailed study of Zuhrīs students and their writings of *ahāith* from him, see *Studies,* pp. 88-93.
17. For detailed study of the subject see, *Studies* p. 302-5.

CHAPTER IV

RECORDING OF *AḤĀDĪTH*

In the previous chapter, I have discussed the methods used by early scholars in teaching and learning the *aḥādīth* of the Prophet.

In seven methods of learning out of eight, from two to eight depend almost totally on the written material. I have also mentioned that the most common were the first and second methods. In many ways, even the first method, that is reading or dictation by the teachers, involved written material in many cases, while the second method, that is reading by students to their teachers required almost exclusively written materials.

However, it is generally believed that the *aḥādīth* were transmitted orally for one hundred years at least. Then Zuhrī recorded them by order of Caliph 'Umar b. 'Abdul 'Azīz. And in the view of some 'scholars', even his recording was lost. Both these assumptions are based on lack of knowledge of the early literary history of *aḥādīth* and their literary style. Therefore the problem of recording of *aḥādīth* needs special attention. Meanwhile it ought to be remembered that mere recording of material is not complete guarantee of its safe preservation. For example, we know that in the existing *Greek Bibles* there are some 200,000 variants, some of them minor and some of them very important, which is sufficient to prove that mere recording of a subject is not a sure guarantee of its safe preservation.[1] However, a text can be kept fully preserved even without recording. For example, even if all the books on the earth were destroyed, the holy Qur'ān would still remain safe because millions of Muslims have memorized it completely or in parts.

Recording of *Ḥadīth* in the Life of the Prophet and the Companions

We know that certain companions wrote down *aḥādīth* in the life of the Prophet and in some cases the Prophet dictated it to them. No doubt their numbers must have been smaller than those of the later scholars who wrote down *aḥādīth*. I will try to give a summary of the work of some Companions who took part in diffusion of *ḥadīth* and devoted great deal of time to it.

1. P. Auvray. A. Barueq etc. *Introduction A La Bible,* P. 111.

It is a well known fact that not all the Companions had equal number of *aḥādīth* for transmission. The proportion of the *aḥādīth* varied. While some of them transmitted more than a thousand most of them transmitted a *ḥadīth* or two only. The names of Companions who transmitted *aḥādīth* in large numbers is as follows: The first name is that of Abū Hurairah, who transmitted, according to Baqī b. Makhalad, 5374 *aḥādīth*. Actually, this is not the number of *hadīth,* but the number of channels through which *aḥādīth* were transmitted. The most recent research shows that the number of *ahādīth* transmitted by him is 1236 only.[2]. He is reported to have had books of *ḥadīth* in his possession. At least nine of Abū Hurairah's students wrote *aḥādīth* from him.

Next to Abū Hurairah comes the name of Ibn 'Umar, who according to Baqī, transmitted 2630 *ḥadīth*[3]. We have authentic reports that he had a written collection of *ḥadīth.* At least eight of his students wrote *aḥādīth* from him. Others who transmitted large numbers of *ḥadīth* were:

Anas ibn Malik, who served the Prophet for ten years and transmitted 2286 *ḥadīth.* At least sixteen persons have *ḥadīth* from him in written form, though some of them are not fully reliable.

Ummul-Mu'minin 'Aisha who transmitted 2210 *ḥadīth.* At least three persons had her *aḥādīth* in written form including her nephew, 'Urwah, one of the greatest scholars amongst the successors.

Ibn 'Abbas, who transmitted 1660 *ḥadīth.* At least nine of his students had *aḥādīth* from him in written form.

Jābir b 'Abdullah who transmitted 1540 *ḥadīth.* At least fourteen of his students had his *aḥādīth* in written form.

Abū Sa'īd al-Khudrī who transmitted 1170 *ḥadīth.* He seems to have been opposed to the writing down of *aḥādīth,* though according to Khatīb he himself wrote a few *aḥādīth.*

Ibn Mas'ūd who transmitted 748 *ḥadīth.* We have no information about his students who wrote down *ḥadīth* from him, but his own book was in the possession of his son.

'Abdullah b. 'Amr b. Al-'Ās, who transmitted 700 *ḥadīth.* We know that he used to write *ḥadīth* while the Prophet was alive and titled his books by

2. Diyā ur-Rahmān al-A'zamī, *Abū Hurairah fī ḍau Mariyātihi,* p. 7, (M.A. Thesis, Sharī'ah College, Mecca).
3. The number of *aḥādīth* mentioned with the names of other Companions do not refer to the actual number of *aḥādīth.* The actual number would be much smaller, as we have seen in the case of Abū Hurairah, but there is no extant study of the subject.

the name of *'al-Ṣahīfah al-Ṣādiqah'*. At least seven of his students have *ḥadīth* from him in written form.

The second Caliph, 'Umar, 537 *aḥādīth* have been transmitted by him. He used to quote *aḥādīth* in official letters and in this way many *ḥadīth* were recorded by him.

The fourth Caliph, 'Alī ibn Abū Ṭālib. He transmitted 536 *aḥādīth*. At least eight of his students had his *ḥadīth* in written form.

Abū Mūsā al-Ash'ari, transmitted 360 *ḥadīth*. Some of his *ḥadīth* were in the possession of Ibn 'Abbās in written form.

Al-Barā' ibn 'Azib, transmitted 305 *ḥadīth*. He used to dictate *ḥadīth*.

I am going to stop at this point, because the instances I have given are sufficient to throw light on the problem under discussion. In the light of above mentioned facts, it is quite safe to assume that probably most of *aḥādīth* of the Prophet, if not all, came to be written during the life of the Companions[4].

Some Misunderstanding About the Recording of *Ḥadīth*.

If what I have written concerning the early recording of *aḥādīth* of the Prophet is correct then how does one explain the general belief that the *aḥādīth* were recorded very late?

I think this mistake is due to the following reasons:

(1) Misinterpretation of the words *Tadwīn, Taṣnīf* and *Kitābah* which were understood in the sense of record.

(2) Misunderstanding of the terms *Haddathanā, Akhbaranā, 'An* etc. which were generally believed to be used for oral transmission.

(3) The claim that the memory of the Arabs was unique and they had no need to write down anything.

(4) Ḥadīth of the Prophet against recording aḥādīth.

(5) Misinterpretation of early scholars' statements concerning recording of *aḥādīth*.

Points four and five need some discussion.

The *Ḥadīth* Against Writing Down the *Aḥādīth*.

In *'Taqyīd al-'Ilm'*, al-Khatīb al Baghdādī deals at full length with the subject of the recording of *aḥādīth* and discusses whether or not it was

---

4. For a detailed study of the problem, see Al Azami, *Studies* p. 34-182.

allowed by the Prophet. The first part of the book is mainly concerned with the disapproval of writing; and the first chapter of this part mainly contains *aḥādīth* from the Prophet, transmitted by Abū Sa'īd al-Khudrī, Abu Huraira and Zaid b.Thābit, forbidding writing of anything except the Qur'ān.

In this first part there are the *aḥādīth* of Abū Sa'īd al Khudrī which had two different versions, one of them transmitted by 'Abd al-Raḥmān b.Zaid. The authorities agree unanimously that he was a weak narrator and according to al-Hākim and Abū Nu'aim he transmitted even false *ahādīth*; and in the words of Ibn Ḥibbān, "He used to reverse *aḥādīth,* without knowing it, and put the full *isnād* for an interrupted (chain), so he deserved to be abandoned". Therefore, the *ḥadīth* of Abū Sa'īd al-Khudrī transmitted by 'Abd al-Rahmān b.Zaid is weak and unacceptable.

The same 'Abd al-Rahmān b.Zaid occurs in the *ḥadīth* of Abū Hurariah. Therefore, this *ḥadīth* is also weak and unacceptable.

The third companion is Zaid by Thābit. His *ḥadīth* is *Mursal.*[5] The transmitter from Zaid is al-Muttalib b.'Abd Allah who did not learn from Zaid, therefore there is a link missing whose honesty is unknown. So this *ḥadīth* is also unacceptable. Furthermore, *ḥadīth* from Zaid has two versions. In one of them, his disapproval of the writing of hadīth is based on the order of the Prophet, while in another statement it is said that he disapproved of it because the written materials were his personal opinions. Therefore, this statement does not confirm his disapproval of the recording of the *aḥādīth* of the Prophet.

There is only one *sahīh ḥadīth* (Trustworthy) transmitted by Abū Sa'īd al-Khudrī, in this matter which reads, "Do not write from me anything except the Qur'ān and whoever has written anything from me other than the Qur'ān should erase it."[6] This *ḥadīth,* which is transmitted by Abū Sa'īd al-Khudrī on the authority of the Prophet is disputed among scholars. According to al-Bukharī and others, it is the statement of Abū Sa'īd himself, that is erroneously attributed to the Prophet, and it actually meant that nothing should be written with the Qur'ān on the same sheet as this might lead someone to conclude erroneously that sentences or words written in the margin or between lines belonged to the Qur'ān. It should be remembered that this command was given when the Qur'ān was being revealed and the text itself was incomplete. Otherwise there does not appear to be any sound reason to forbid the writing of *aḥādīth.*

5. For the explanation of the term, see, below, p. **64**
6. Mu.*Zuhd,* 72.

The Prophet himself sent hundreds of letters. Many of them were lengthy, containing the formulae for forms and rituals of worship. According to the Qur'ān his conduct and deeds should be followed by the community. The Qur'ān itself demands a record of financial transactions. Therefore, it looks as if there were no general instructions not to record the *aḥādīth,* though it might have been understood by some of the Scholars in this way. On the other hand there is clear evidence to show that the Prophet approved of recording the *aḥādīth.* Furthermore, we find that quite a number of Companions recorded *aḥādīth* and among them were also those people who transmitted *ḥadīth* which forbade its recording. Bearing all this in mind one arrives at the conclusion that the prophet's disapproval of writing down *aḥādīth* most probably meant the writing of the Qur'ān and non-Qur'ānic material on the same sheet because that might have led to misunderstanding.

There is another theory that it was forbidden to write down *aḥādīth* in early days because all attention should be paid to the Qur'ān and its preservation, and later on, when there was no danger of neglecting the Qur'ān, the previous order was abrogated and people were permitted to write down *aḥādīth.*[7]

Misinterpretation of Early Scholars' Statements.

There have been many scholars who wrote down *aḥādīth,* and sometimes disliked doing so, giving reasons for their attitudes which were not based on the Prophet's teachings. In many cases, the reasons were omitted, or even when the statements were given in full they were interpreted as against writing without any serious consideration.

Some Examples

1. It is reported that Ibrāhīm al-Nakha'ī was against writing. The reason he gave for disapproval was that "whoever writes becomes dependent on it." According to the conception of some early scholars, books were bad stores of knowledge, and the best store was one which is kept in memory which could be used anywhere and at any time. One of the Bedouin said: a word in your memory is better than ten in your book.
2. The name of 'Amir al-Sha'bī has been given in the lists of those against writing. If one reads his statement carefully one must reach the conclusion that al-Sha'bī was not against writing. We have two of

7. For detailed discussion, see Al-Azami, *Studies in Early Ḥadīth literature* p. 18-27.

his statements on the subject. In one of them he says, "I neither wrote with black on white nor did I ask any man to repeat a *ḥadīth* twice to me". The purpose of this statement is to show his great power of memory so that he never needed to ask anyone to repeat a *ḥadīth* and to hear it only once was sufficient for him to memorize it. The statement has no connection with the subject of the recording of *ḥadīth*. In another statement he advises his students to write down everything they hear from him; if they did not have paper they were even asked to write on walls.

No doubt there were some scholars who disliked the writing down of *Ḥadīth* at one time or another for reasons which were not based on any religious authority.

The most famous scholar during the late first and early second century was Zuhrī, who had written down almost everything which he had heard from his teachers. But when he began to teach he did not agree to dictate the *aḥādīth,* till pressure was exerted on him through the Caliph Hishām.[8] Why was it so? To understand the reason thoroughly we need to see it in his own statement as well as of Mālik b.Anas who was the student of Zuhrī. One of the students of Mālik read *al-Muwaṭṭā'* to him in forty days, upon which Mālik said: The knowledge which I have collected in forty years you are gaining in forty days. How little can you understand it![9] Perhaps he wanted to say: How little can you appreciate it. Once al-Sha'bī transmitted a *ḥadīth,* then said to the student that you are really getting it for nothing, otherwise even for less one had to make a journey from Iraq to al-Madīnā.[10] Actually it was the general attitude of that time that the teachers could hardly be brought to speak. The students had to accompany them and when their teachers spoke, they wrote it down or memorized it. Zuhrī says: "People used to sit with Ibn'Umar but none dared call upon him till someone (from outside) came and asked him. We sat with Ibn al-Musayyab without questioning him, till someone came and questioned him, the question roused him to impart *ḥadīth* to us, or he began to impart of his own will".[11] Therefore, although al-Zuhrī wrote down *ḥadīth* for his own use, he was not in favour of making them public. One who wants to learn must strive, and the student should not be given any ready-made knowledge in the shape of a book or dictation.

8. Abū Nu'aim, *al-Hilya,* iii, 363.
9. al-Zurqānī, *Shārh al-Muwaṭṭā,'* i.7.
10. al-Khatīb, *al-Riḥlah,* 61-62.
11. For detail see, Azami, *Studies,* 284.

Summing up the argument regarding the reasons for disliking recording, there is no evidence that the interdiction of writing was based on the order of the Prophet. It was based at one time or another on personal prejudice. Nevertheless the same scholars committed *aḥādīth* to writing. The recent research has proved that almost all the *ḥadīth* of the Prophet was written down in the life of Companions, which stretched to the end of the first century.

If the recording is carried out for the preservation of recorded material, then no doubt *aḥādīth* were preserved in this way. However, due to unique theory of learning which I have described in the chapter on *Taḥammul al-'Ilm,* direct approach to these books by everyone was regarded improper. It had to be through scholars authorized by proper teachers. These scholars themselves became part of the information and cannot be separated from it. In other words, sources of information became essential part of information, without which the information had no value. These sources of information are called *isnād,* the chain of the transmitters. In the next chapter we shall discuss the problem of *isnād.*

CHAPTER V

ISNĀD SYSTEM (CHAIN OF TRANSMITTERS)

Every *ḥadīth* consists of two parts. Here is a *ḥadīth* quoted from Bukhārī.

Bukhārī said that Sulaimān Abū ar-Rabī' informed him saying that Ismā'īl b. Ja'far said that Nāfi' b. Mālik informed him on the authority of his father that Abū Huraira related that the Prophet said: the signs of a Hypocrite are three;

Whenever he speaks he tells a lie.
Whenever he makes a promise, he breaks it.
Whenever trusted with something he proves to be dishonest.

This *ḥadīth* contains a series of names of narrators, and then the actual subject relating to the Prophet.

The first portion is called *isnād* while the actual statement or information relating to the Prophet is called *matn*. *Isnād*, according to Arabic lexicography means the thing on which another relies. As we rely on the narrators for the knowledge of the statement of the Prophet, this chain is called *isnād*. Its plural is *asānīd*. Sometimes the term *ṭarīq* is used instead of *isnād*, and sometimes the term *wajh* is used for the same purpose.

Origins of *Isnād*

It appears that *isnād* was used casually in some literature in Pre-Islamic period in a vague manner, without attaching any importance to it. The *isnād* system was also used to some extent in transmitting pre-Islamic poetry.[1] But it was in the *ḥadīth* literature that its importance culminated till it was counted as part of the religion.[2] The system was used to the full, and in some cases to extravagant limits, for documenting the *hadīth* literature,—the store room for the *sunna*. The *sunna* of the Prophet being a basic legal source, it was natural to deal with these documents with utmost care. Thus with the introduction of *isnād*, a unique science *'Ilm*

1. Nāṣir al-Asad, *Maṣādir al-Shi'r al-Jāhilī*, 255-267.
2. MU. *Introduction*, pp. 14-16.

al-Jarḥ wa al-Ta'dil came into existence for the evaluation of *isnād* and *aḥādīth*.

I have described earlier that it was the common practice among Companions—even in the life of the Prophet—to transmit the *aḥādīth* of the Prophet, when they saw each other. Some of them had even made special arrangements to attend the Prophet's circle in shifts and to inform each other of what they had heard and seen in the presence of the Prophet.

Naturally in informing their fellows they would have used sentences like: 'the Prophet did such and such' or 'the Prophet said so and so'. It is also natural that one of them who had gained knowledge at second hand, while reporting the incident to a third man, might have disclosed his sources of information and might have given the full account of the incident. There are ample references of this kind in the *Ḥadīth literature*. Only one will be quoted here.

Dimām b.Tha'labah came to the Prophet and said to him: "Muhammed, your messenger came to us and told us . . .".[3] These methods, which were used in the early days for the diffusion of the *sunna* of the Prophet, gave birth to *'isnād'*, and this was the rudimentary beginning of the system. In this regard Ibn Sīrīn's statement would be very helpful. He says, "They did not ask about the *isnād,* but when civil war—*Fitnah*—arose they said 'Name to us your men; those who belong to *Ahl-al-Sunnah,* their *aḥādīth* were accepted and those who were innovators their *aḥādīth* were neglected."[4]

This gives the impression that the *isnād* was used even before the *Fitnah,* but the narrators were not so perfect in applying it. Sometimes they employed it and at others neglected it. After the civil war they became more cautious and began to enquire about the sources of information and scrutinized them. At the end of the first century the science of the *isnād* was fully developed. Shu'bah used to watch the lips of Qatādah, in the lecture, to discriminate between his first and second hand information. There are ample references to asking and enquiring about the *isnād* in the first century of the Hijrah.

The Proliferation of *Isnāds*

It is a common phenomenon of *isnād* system that as we go further in time the number of transmitters increases. Sometimes a *ḥadīth* transmitted by one companion acquires ten students in the next generation, in the class

---

3. MU, *Imān,* 10.
4. MU, *Introduction,* 15.

of Successors, and in turn these ten students have in some cases twenty or thirty students belonging to different countries and provinces.

I give here a few examples to show how the *isnād* proliferated.

Example 1:

Abū Hurairah reported that Rasūlullah صلى الله عليه وسلم said when anyone amongst you wakes up from sleep, he must not put his hand in a utensil till he has washed it three times, for he does not know where his hand was during sleep.

At least thirteen students of Abū Hurairah transmitted this *ḥadīth* from him.

8 out of 13 were from Madīnah.
1 was from Kūfah.
2 from Baṣrah.
1 from Yemen.
1 from Syria.

There are sixteen scholars who transmitted this *ḥadīth* from the students of Abū Hurairah.

6 out of 16 were from Madīnah.
4 from Baṣrah.
2 from Kūfah, Iraq.
1 from Makkah.
1 from Yemen.
1 from Khurāsān.
1 from Hims (Syria).

Example 2:

حد ثنا عبد العزيز بن المختار قال حد ثنا سهيل بن ابى صالح عن أبيه عن أبى هريرة أن النبى صلى الله عليه وسلم قال : انما الا مام ليؤتم به اذا كبر فكبروا ، واذا ركع فاركعوا واذا قال سمع الله لمن حمده فقولوا : اللهم ربنا لك الحمد ، واذا سجد فاسجدوا ولا تسجدوا حتى يسجد ، واذا رفع فارفعوا ولا ترفعوا حتى يرفع ، واذا صلى قاعدا فصلوا قعودا أجمعون .

Abū Huraira reported the Prophet saying: The *Imām* ought to be followed. So recite *takbīr* when he recites and bow down when he bows

Here is the chart of this *Ḥadīth* upto the time of the classical authors.

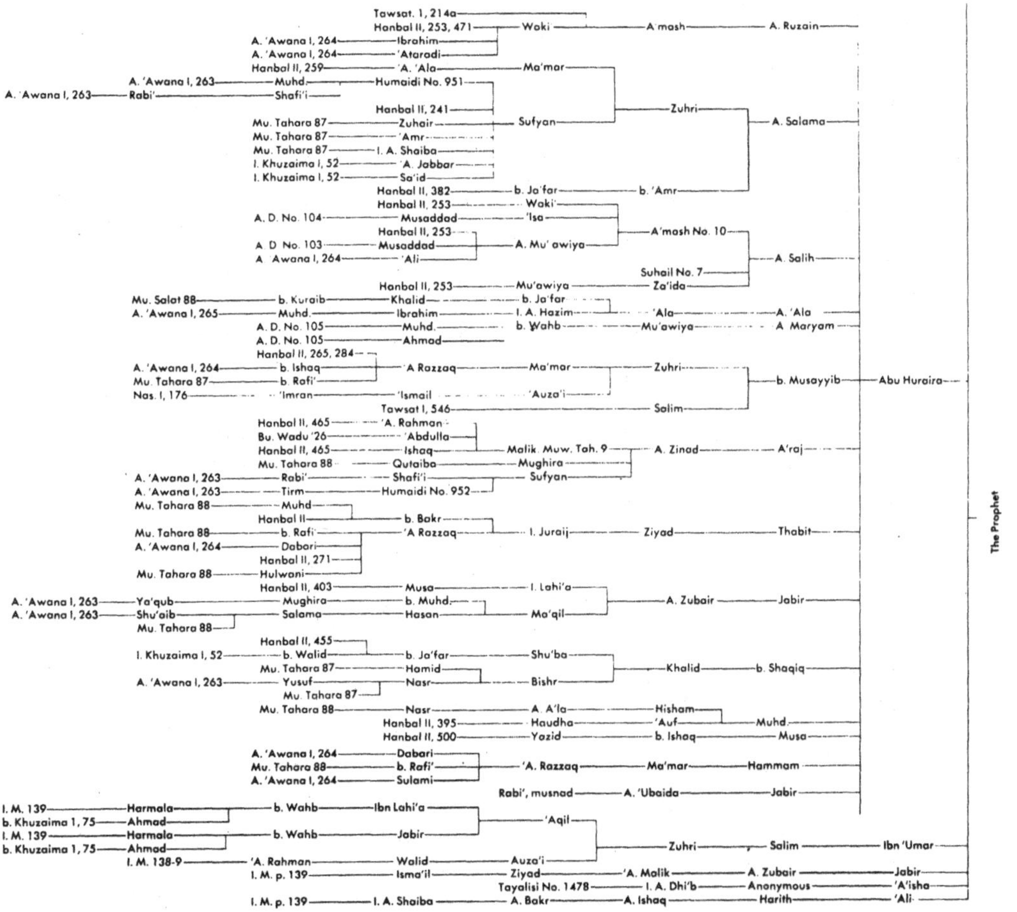

down. And when he says: سمع الله لمن حمده "Allah listens to him who praises Him", say اللهم ربنا لك الحمد

"O Allah, our Lord, to thee be praise". And when he prostrates, you should prostrate. You must not prostrate till he prostrates. When he raises (his head) you should raise yours. You must not raise your head till he raises. If he prays sitting, all of you should pray sitting.

This *ḥadīth* is reported by twenty six third generation authorities, all of whom trace the origins of their knowledge to Companions of the Prophet. It is found almost in the same form or in the same meaning in all versions in ten different locations at this time (Madīna, Makka, Egypt, Baṣrah, Hims,

Yemen, Kūfa, Syria, Wāsiṭ and Ṭā'if). Three of the twenty six authorities heard it from more than one source.

Existing documentation shows that this *ḥadīth* was transmitted by at least ten Companions. We have details of the courses of transmission for seven of these ten, showing that they came originally from three different places—Madina, Syria and Iraq.

The course of transmission from only one of the Companions—Abū Hurairah—shows clearly how the number of transmitters increased from generation to generation and how the *ḥadīth* became known in widely different locations. Abū Hurairah had at least seven students who transmitted this *ḥadīth* from him. Four of these belonged to Madīna, two to Egypt and one to Yemen. These students in turn transmitted to at least twelve others—five from Madīna, two from Makka and one each from Syria, Kufa, Tā'if, Egypt and Yemen.

Similar patterns of transmission from the other Companions show how the *ḥadīth* spread wider—to Baṣrah, Himṣ and Wāsiṭ—and reinforced the *ḥadīth* in Madīna, Makka, Kufa, Egypt and Syria.

Example 3:

> Abū Huraira reported the Prophet saying that Almighty Allah said: "Every act of the son of Adam is for him, a good deed would be rewarded tenfold, except fasting which is (exclusively) meant for Me, and I (alone) will reward it. One abandons his food for My sake and abandons drinking for My sake, and abandons his pleasure for My sake. When any one of you is fasting he should neither indulge in sex nor use obscene language. If anyone reviles him he should say, I am fasting. The one who fasts has two (occasions) of joy: one when he breaks the fast and one the day when he would meet his Lord.
>
> And the breath (of one who fasts) is sweeter to Allah than the fragrance of musk."

This lengthy *ḥadīth* has been transmitted by many scholars in parts. Ibn Ḥanbal has endorsed it at least twenty-four times. It is included in the collections of A'mash (d. 148), Ibn Juraij (d. 150) and Ibrāhīm b. Tahmān (d. 168)—transmitters from the students of Abū Hurairah. It is also found in Shi'ite, Zaidī and Ibādī sources.

If we confine the discussion only to the third generation of narrators from Abū Hurairah, belonging mostly to the first half of the second century of the *Hijrah*, the following features appear: There are twenty-two third generation transmitters—nine from Madīna, five from Baṣrah, four from

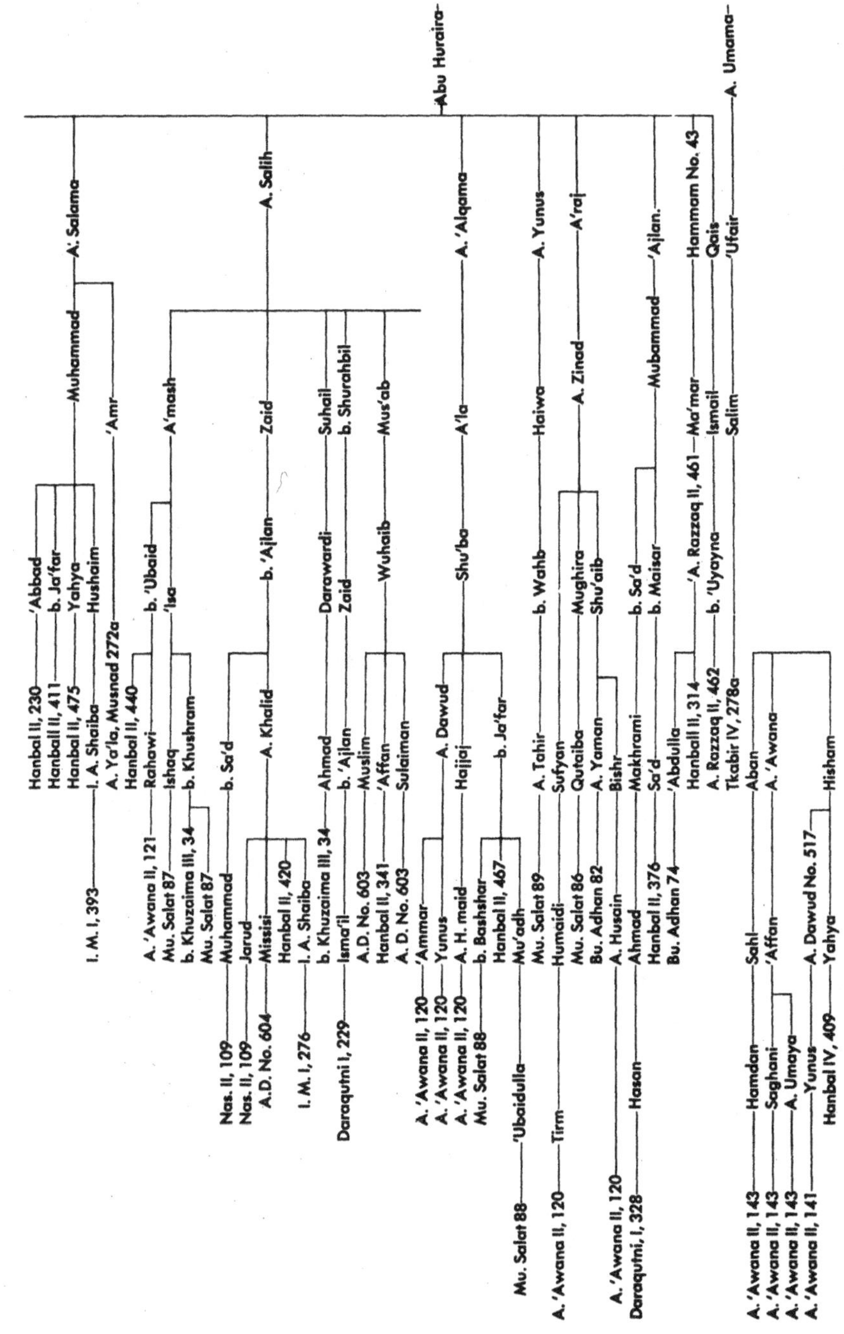
Abu Huraira
A. Umama
A. Salama
Muhammad
'Amr
'Abbad
b. Ja'far
Yahya
Hushaim
Hanbal II, 230
Hanbal II, 411
Hanbal II, 475
I. A. Shaiba
I. M. I, 393
A. Ya'la, Musnad 272a
Hanbal II, 440
A. Salih
A'mash
b. 'Ubaid
'Isa
Rahawi
Ishaq
b. Khushram
A. 'Awana II, 121
Mu. Salat 87
b. Khuzaima III, 34
Mu. Salat 87
Zaid
b. 'Ajlan
b. Sa'd
A. Khalid
Muhammad
Jarud
Missisi
Hanbal II, 420
I. A. Shaiba
Nas. II, 109
Nas. II, 109
A.D. No. 604
I. M. I, 276
Suhail
b. Shurahbil
Mus'ab
Darawardi
Zaid
Wuhaib
Ahmad
b. 'Ajlan
Muslim
'Affan
Sulaiman
b. Khuzaima III, 34
Isma'il
A.D. No. 603
Hanbal II, 341
A. D. No. 603
Daraqutni I, 229
A. 'Alqama
A'la
Shu'ba
A. Dawud
Hajjaj
b. Ja'far
'Ammar
Yunus
A. H. maid
b. Bashshar
Hanbal II, 467
Mu'adh
A. 'Awana II, 120
A. 'Awana II, 120
A. 'Awana II, 120
Mu. Salat 88
'Ubaidulla
Mu. Salat 88
A. Yunus
Haiwa
b. Wahb
A. Tahir
Mu. Salat 89
A'raj
A. Zinad
Mughira
Shu'aib
Sufyan
Qutaiba
A. Yaman
Bishr
Humaidi
Mu. Salat 86
Bu. Adhan 82
A. Husain
Tirm
A. 'Awana II, 120
A. 'Awana II, 120
'Ajlan.
Mubammad
b. Sa'd
b. Maisar
Makhrami
Sa'd
'Abdulla
Ahmad
Hanbal II, 376
Bu. Adhan 74
Hasan
Daraqutni, I, 328
Hammam No. 43
Ma'mar
'A. Razzaq II, 461
Hanbal II, 314
Qais
Ismail
b. 'Uyayna
A. Razzaq II, 462
'Ufair
Salim
Tkabir IV, 278a
Aban
A. 'Awana
Hisham
Sahl
'Affan
A. Dawud No. 517
Yahya
Hamdan
Saghani
A. Umaya
Yunus
Hanbal IV, 409
A. 'Awana II, 143
A. 'Awana II, 143
A. 'Awana II, 143
A. 'Awana II, 141

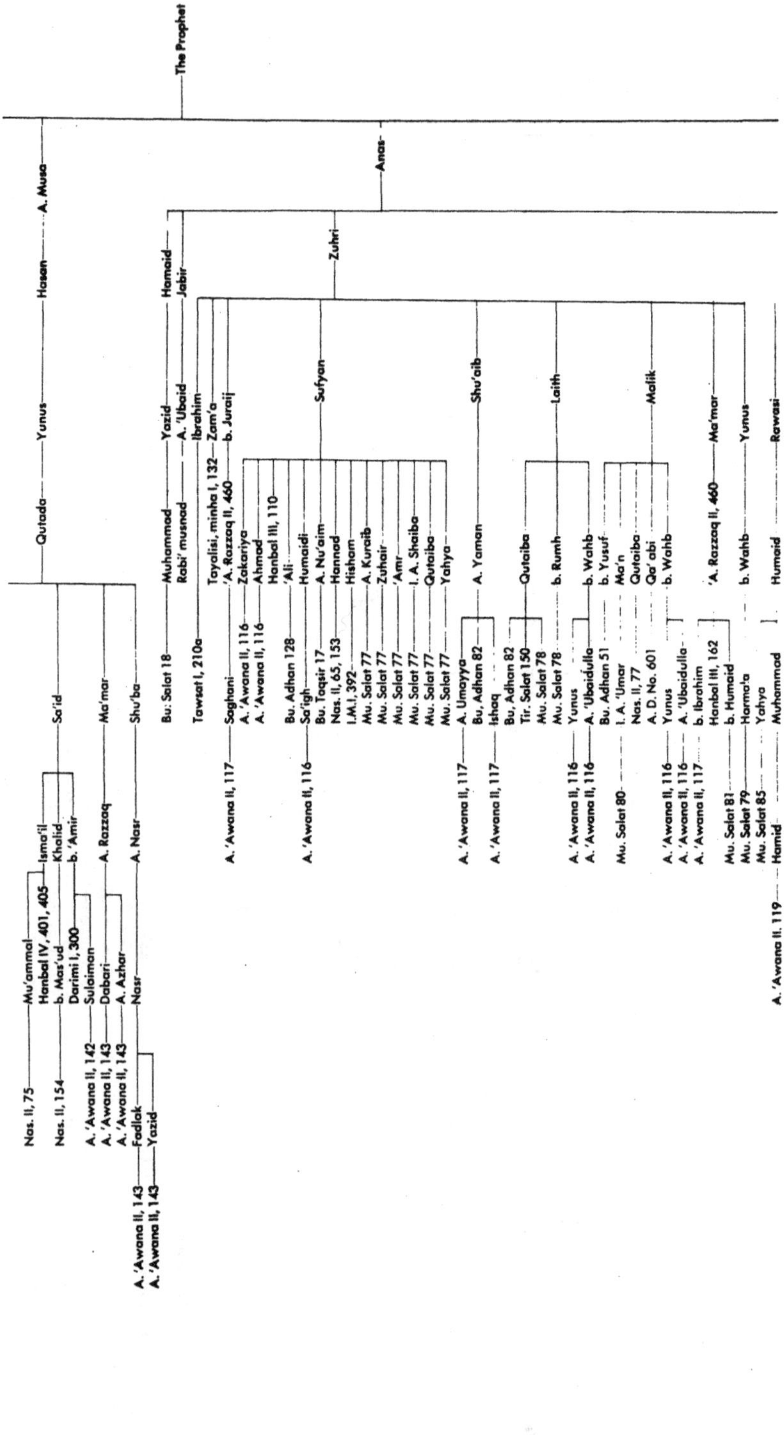
The Prophet
A. Musa
Hasan
Yunus
Qatada
Sa'id
Ma'mar
Shu'ba
Mu'ammal
Isma'il
Hanbal IV, 401, 405
Khalid
b. Mas'ud
b. 'Amir
Darimi I, 300
Sulaiman
A. Razzaq
Dabari
A. Azhar
A. Nasr
Nasr
Nas. II, 75
Nas. II, 154
A. 'Awana II, 142
A. 'Awana II, 143
A. 'Awana II, 143
Fadlak
Yazid
A. 'Awana II, 143
A. 'Awana II, 143
Anas
Zuhri
Hamaid
Jabir
Yazid
A. 'Ubaid
Muhammad
Rabi' musnad
Bu: Salat 18
Ibrahim
Zam'a
b. Juraij
Tayalisi, minha I, 132
'A. Razzaq II, 460
Tawsat I, 210a
Sufyan
Shu'aib
Laith
Malik
Ma'mar
Yunus
Rawasi
Zakariya
Ahmad
Hanbal III, 110
'Ali
Humaidi
A. Nu'aim
Hannad
Hisham
A. Kuraib
Zuhair
'Amr
I. A. Shaiba
Qutaiba
Yahya
Saghani
A. 'Awana II, 116
A. 'Awana II, 116
Bu. Adhan 128
Sa'igh
Bu. Tagsir 17
Nas. II, 65, 153
I.M.I, 392
Mu. Salat 77
Mu. Salat 77
Mu. Salat 77
Mu. Salat 77
Mu. Salat 77
Mu. Salat 77
A. 'Awana II, 117
A. 'Awana II, 116
A. Yaman
A. Umayya
Bu. Adhan 82
Ishaq
A. 'Awana II, 117
A. 'Awana II, 117
Qutaiba
Bu. Adhan 82
Tir. Salat 150
Mu. Salat 78
Mu. Salat 78
b. Rumh
b. Wahb
Yunus
A. 'Ubaidulla
A. 'Awana II, 116
A. 'Awana II, 116
b. Yusuf
Ma'n
Qutaiba
Qa' abi
b. Wahb
Bu. Adhan 51
I. A. 'Umar
Nas. II, 77
A. D. No. 601
Mu. Salat 80
Yunus
A. 'Ubaidulla
b. Ibrahim
A. 'Awana II, 116
A. 'Awana II, 116
A. 'Awana II, 117
'A. Razzaq II, 460
Hanbal III, 162
b. Wahb
b. Humaid
Harma'a
Yahya
Mu. Salat 81
Mu. Salat 79
Mu. Salat 85
Humaid
Muhammad
Hamid
A. 'Awana II. 119

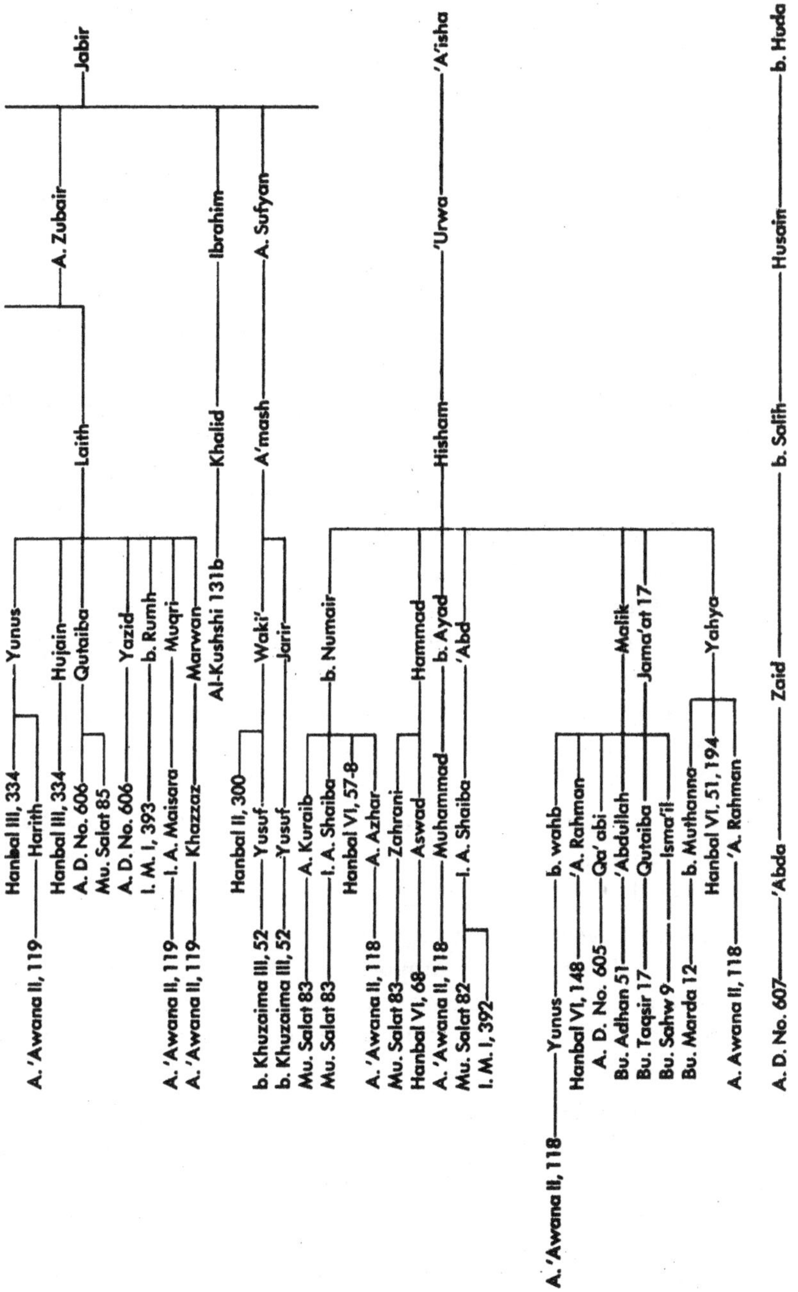
Jabir
A. Zubair
Laith
Yunus
Hanbal III, 334
Harith
A. 'Awana II, 119
Hujain
Hanbal III, 334
Qutaiba
A. D. No. 606
Mu. Salat 85
Yazid
A. D. No. 606
b. Rumh
I. M. I, 393
Muqri
I. A. Maisara
A. 'Awana II, 119
Marwan
Khazzaz
A. 'Awana II, 119
Ibrahim
Khalid
Al-Kushshi 131b
A. Sufyan
A'mash
Waki'
Hanbal II, 300
Yusuf
b. Khuzaima III, 52
Jarir
Yusuf
b. Khuzaima III, 52
b. Numair
A. Kuraib
Mu. Salat 83
I. A. Shaiba
Mu. Salat 83
Hanbal VI, 57-8
A. Azhar
A. 'Awana II, 118
'A'isha
'Urwa
Hisham
Hammad
Zahrani
Mu. Salat 83
Aswad
Hanbal VI, 68
b. Ayad
Muhammad
A. 'Awana II, 118
'Abd
I. A. Shaiba
Mu. Salat 82
I. M. I, 392
Malik
b. wahb
Yunus
A. 'Awana II, 118
'A. Rahman
Hanbal VI, 148
Qa' abi
A. D. No. 605
'Abdullah
Bu. Adhan 51
Jama'at 17
Qutaiba
Bu. Taqsir 17
Isma'il
Bu. Sahw 9
Yahya
b. Muthanna
Bu. Marda 12
Hanbal VI, 51, 194
'A. Rahman
A. Awana II, 118
b. Huda
Husain
b. Salih
Zaid
'Abda
A. D. No. 607

Kūfa, and one each from Makka, Wāsiṭ, Hijāz and Khurāsān. These variously trace their source to eleven students of Abū Hurairah, whose homes were in Madīna, Baṣra and Kūfa.

Without going into details, however, I draw a diagram for this *ḥadīth* to show how easy it was for *ḥadīth* knowledge to spread throughout the Islamic world and how the number of transmitters, in most cases, increased in each generation.

Further down the chain, the number of narrators increases and localities spread even further into different provinces. The flourishing of *isnād* and diffusion of *aḥādīth* in this way made it easy to check the faults of scholars, or any forgery that was committed. This proves the early existence of the *isnād* system and shows how impossible it would have been to fabricate *isnāds* on this large scale.

A second interesting point is that not all the Madinese, Basrites or Kufans are the students of one man. Three of the Basrites trace the source of their knowledge to one Basrite, but the other two cite two different Madinese as their source. The Chart of the *Isnad* of this *Hadith* is on Page 41

The illustrations serve to show how well documented are the *isnāds* of the majority of *aḥādīth,* how the system is used in examining the statements of scholars, and how it was and can be used for eliminating mistakes.

No doubt not all the *aḥādīth* were spread so widely. There are *aḥādīth* which were transmitted—according to our available sources—through a single scholar from a single scholar for three or four generations.

Here is an example: وقال ابو هريرة، قال النبي صلى الله عليه وسلم، "اذا صليت الجمعة فصل بعدها أربعاً"

Abū Huraira reported the Prophet صلى الله عليه وسلم

saying that whenever you pray *Jum'a,* pray four *rak'a* after it. Chart P.42.

Now we have almost a complete picture of the spreading of *isnād.* These charts cited above provide support for complete confidence in the system of *isnād* and its beginning from the time of the Prophet. It was impossible to fabricate on this great a scale in an era lacking the modern facilities of communication.

I described in the previous chapter the efforts made by early scholars to distinguish between valid and invalid *aḥādīth,* and the rigorous methods they used to examine chains of transmission, eliminating all *aḥādīth* passed on by unreliable sources. Given centuries of this kind of activity, we are logically justified in accepting the whole system of *isnād* and methodology of *ḥadīth* scholars as accurate and valid.

Here is the chart of the *isnād* of this *ḥadīth*

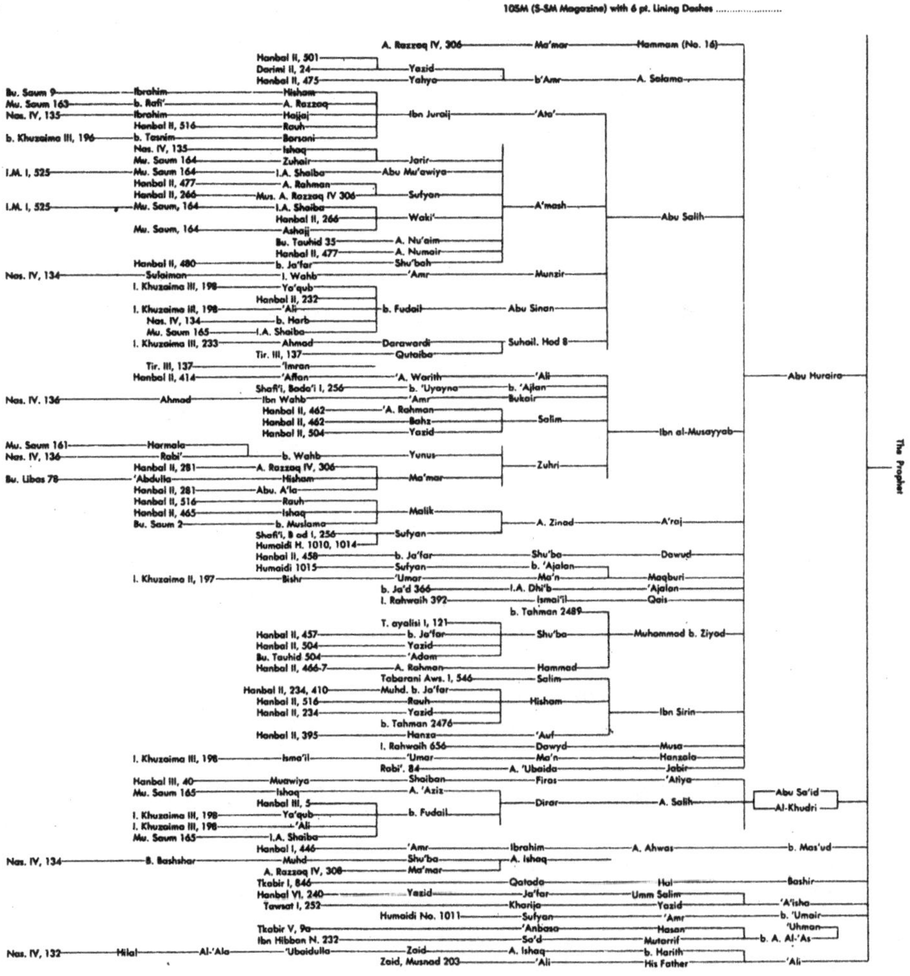

Here is the chart.

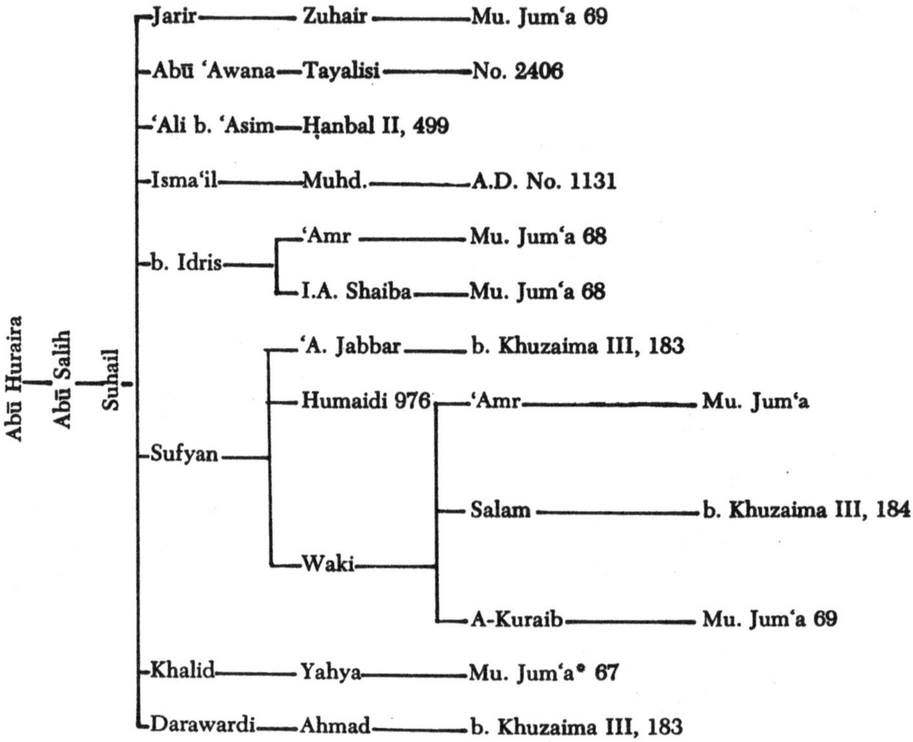

Isnād and Its Impact on Classification of *Aḥādīth*

A common feature of a good many *aḥādīth* in the early part of the second century A.H., as is evident from the charts, is the great number of transmitters who belong to different provinces and countries. However, not all the *aḥādīth* had the one pattern in the spread of *isnād.* We have seen that some of the *aḥādīth* were transmitted by many Companions and many many successors[5] while some others were related by a single Companion only from whom it was narrated by a single Successor, who in turn had a single student who transmitted this particular *ḥadīth.*[6]

Therefore *aḥādīth* were graded according to the numbers of narrators. In this regard the following terms need attention: a. *Mutawātir,* b. *'Ahād.*

5. For examples, see page diagrams No. 1-3.
6. For example, see page diagram No. 4.

Mutawātir: report of a large number of narrators whose agreement upon a lie is inconceivable. This condition must be met in the entire chain from the origins of the report to the very end.

In the view of Muslim scholars any *ḥadīth* which has been transmitted by *tawātur* and whose reporters based their reports on direct, unambiguous, perception unmixed with rationalization would produce knowledge with certainty.

However, there is a difference of opinion about the required number of narrators for *mutawātir ḥadīth,* ranging from four to several hundreds.

In my opinion if a *ḥadīth* was transmitted by a few Companions, say four for example, and everyone of them had a number of students scattered throughout the Muslim world and in course of transmission their number increased and their locality varied more and more, even this small number would produce the knowledge with certainty, especially for those people who knew the character of early scholars.

a.) *Mutawātir* has been divided in two groups:

1. *Mutawātir* by words,.
2. *Mutawātir* in the meaning.

Only a few *aḥādīth* have been mentioned as *Mutawāir* by words, meaning all the narrators used the same expression. However, *mutawātir* in the sense and meanings are numerous.

b.) *'Āḥād,* whose narrators do not reach anywhere near the number for *mutawātir*. It has been divided into many sub-divisions. Some of them are as below.[7]

Al-Mashhūr: (well-known) That is a *ḥadīth* transmitted by three or more transmitters in every stage.

Al-'Azīz: That is a *ḥadīth* transmitted at least by two narrators in every generation.

Al-Gharīb: If an *isnād* had a single narrator either throughout its *isnād*—after the Companion—or in any stage, it is called *Gharīb*.

Al-Fard which has been divided into two sub-divisions:

a) *Fard mutlaq,* which means that this particular *ḥadīth* was transmitted by that particular person alone.

b) *Fard Nisbī,* which has several meanings:

i) None of the trustworthy transmitters narrated that particular *ḥadith* except that particular person (narrator); or others narrated it as well but they were not trustworthy.

7. Sometimes more than one definition has been given by the scholars. However, I have mentioned only one that is accepted by the majority of the scholars.

ii) None of the people of other regions transmitted that particular *ḥadīth* except the scholars of that particular region.

Marfū': That is *isnād* of the *ḥadīth* goes back to the Prophet, though it might be broken somewhere.

Musnad: That is *isnād* of the *ḥadīth* is uninterrupted and goes back to the Prophet.

Muttasil: That is *isnād* of the *ḥadīth* is unbroken.

Mauqūf: The *isnād* of *hadīth* goes back to the Companion only.

Maqṭū': A *ḥadīth* going back to the Successor only.

Mursal: Transmission of a Successor from the Prophet directly dropping the Companion from the *Isnād.*

Mu'allaq: An *isnād* in which one or more authorities from the beginning (from the author or book) is omitted.

Munqaṭi': An *isnād* having a single link missing somewhere in the middle, in one place or more.

Mu'ḍal: An *isnād* in which two continuous links are missing in one or more than one places.

Mu'an'an: In the *isnād,* in transmitting the material the term *'an* has been used, which is not explicit in describing the method of receiving the *ḥadīth.*

Musalsal: Is a *ḥadīth* all of whose narrators had a similar situation. For example all of them used same terminology in narration such as *Sami'tu.* Or all of them belong to one region or one occupation. Or they narrated the *ḥadīth* with the same action, e.g. all the narrators smiled while narrating a *ḥadīth* because the Prophet had smiled while saying it.

Al-Ḥadīth al-Qudsī

Some of the *aḥādīth* are narrated by the Prophet, saying that Almighty Allah says so and so. These *ahādīth* are called *Ḥadīth Qudsī.* The meaning of these *ahādīth* was revealed to the Prophet who put them in his own expression. The Holy Qur'ān is the real word of Almighty Allah and the Prophet had only to receive it and then to teach it to the people, explain it and act accordingly. However, other *aḥādīth* which are not called *Qudsī* cannot be said to be totally uninspired by Allah. The Prophet was never left unguided by Allah. Even his *ijtihādāt* were sanctioned by Allah and in case of any lack of clarity it was corrected by Him. Therefore a good deal of *aḥādīth* are *Qudsī* in a sense, but cannot be distinguished from the ones which belong to *ijtihādāt* of the Prophet. Thus we simply have to name them *ahādīth*, being the possibility of *ijtihādāt* of the Prophet. An example of *Ḥadīth-Qudsī:*

> Abu Dharr reported Allah's Messenger صلى الله عليه وسلم as saying that Allah, the Exalted and Glorious, said: My servants, I have made oppression unlawful for Me and unlawful for you, so do not commit oppression against one another. My servants, all of you are liable to err except one whom I guide on the right path, so seek right guidance from Me so that I should direct you to the right path. O My servants, all of you are hungry (needy) except one whom I feed, so beg food from Me, so that I may give that to you. O My servants, all of you are naked (need clothes) except one whom I provide garments, so beg clothes from Me, so that I should clothe you. O My servants, you commit error night and day and I am there to pardon your sins, so beg pardon from Me so that I should grant you pardon. O My servants, you can neither do Me any harm nor can you do Me any good. O My servants, even if the first amongst you and the last amongst you and even the whole of the human race of yours, and that of Jinns even, become (equal in) God-consciousness like the heart of a single person amongst you, nothing would add to My power. O My servants, even if the first amongst you and the last amongst you and the whole human race of yours and that of Jinns too in unison become the most wicked (all beating) like the heart of a single person, it would cause no loss to My Power. O My servants, even if the first amongst you and the last amongst you and the whole human race of yours and that of Jinns also all stand in one plain ground and ask Me and I confer upon every person what he asks for, it would not, in any way, cause any loss to Me (even less) than that which is caused to the ocean by dipping the needle in it. My servants, these deeds of your which I am recording for you I shall reward you for them, so he who finds good shall praise Allah and he who does not find that should not blame anyone but his ownself.[8]

These are some of the classifications of *aḥādīth* basing on the various condition of *isnād*. But there is another classification of *aḥādīth*, different from these, which basically concern acceptance or rejection of *aḥādīth*. This classification came into existence due to criticism carried out by *Muḥad-dithīn*. In the next chapters we will discuss the history and methodology of *hadīth* criticism, and later on its grading and classification.

8. MU. *Birr*, 55.

CHAPTER VI

ḤADĪTH CRITICISM HISTORY AND METHODOLOGY

I have pointed out the fact that all the problems concerning *Hadīth* of the Prophet rest upon the central question of the status of the *sunna,* or we may say *Ḥadīth,* of the Prophet which is the second main source of Islamic law, valid forever, and the life of the Prophet is a model which ought to be followed by Muslims irrespective of time and place. For this reason, the Companions, even in the life of the Prophet, began to diffuse the knowledge of the *sunna* and they were ordered by the Prophet to do so. However, this does not mean that the door was wide open for everybody to transmit the *Ḥadīth* even if he was sure that he was not committing a mistake. The Prophet warned the people saying: "If anyone tells a lie about me intentionally, let him be sure of his place in hell fire."[1]

In another *Ḥadīth,* he said: "If anyone intentionally ascribes to me what I have not said, then let him be sure of his place in Hell-Fire."[2] These warnings produced tremendous effect on the Companions of the Prophet. Many Companions refrained from imparting *Ḥadīth* in case of doubtful memory. In this regard one may give examples of Anas b. Mālik[3], Zubair b. al-'awwā[4], Suhaib[5], Zaid b. arqam[6], as well as 'Abdullah Ibn 'Umar[7].

We find certain Companions checking other Companions, asking them to be very sure and precise as to what they related, on the authority of the Prophet.

---

1. BU. *'Ilm,* 38.
2. *Ibid.*
3. *Ibid.*
4. *Ibid.,* 3.
5. Al-Balādhuri, *Ansāb,* 1.138.
6. I.M. *Introd.* 3.
7. Ḥanbal, iv, 433.

Forgery and Errors in Transmitting of *Aḥādīth*

Scholars, especially early scholars, played their roles with due caution in transmitting or copying *aḥādīth*. But, as is known to all scholars, even the most sincere one may commit a mistake at one time or another.

As the *sunna* of the Prophet is an everlasting example for the Muslim Community, the community, too, cannot afford to let it be polluted or diluted in any way. Therefore, to check mistakes of all sorts, it was necessary to use criticism with full force. The following incidents throw some light on this point.

Yaḥyā b. Sa'īd al-Qaṭṭān, one of the greatest scholars of the second century was on his death bed. He asked one of the attendants, "what do the people of Baṣra say about me?" He replied, "They admire you, but they are only afraid of your criticism of the scholars." On which, he said, "Listen to me, in the Hereafter I would prefer to be opposed by anyone rather than have the Prophet saying: 'You heard a *ḥadīth* attributed to me, and it came to your mind that it was not true but you did not criticize it.' "[8]

With this intention the criticism of *Ḥadīth* was carried out, without fear or favor. One finds that a father graded down his own son, a son criticized his father, a brother criticized his own kin and friends criticized their dear one without any fear or favor except the fear of Allah. I think this is very hard to appreciate in the 20th Century, because respect for father or brother or love of children has become minimal, but anyone who knows the early history and knows how tight the social unit was, and that it was almost impossible to live cut off from the family and family honor, would realize how courageous *muḥaddithīn* were in this respect.

The other point which needs clarification is that in real-life experience we find people always grading their friends higher and lowering the grades of their opponents. Could that have happened in the grading done by *muḥaddithīn?* It could have because this is human weakness and *muḥaddithīn* were human beings. They tried their best to be objective yet there are some traces here and there which indicate that personal enmity played some part in grading lower. The scholars have discussed the subject as well as the case where it was committed. But apart from the exceptions the opposite is true.

Naqd al-Hadīth: Criticism of *Ḥadīth*

In Arabic literature, the word *naqad* is used for criticism. This word was used by some early scholars of *Ḥadīth* in the Second century.[9]

8. Ibn. Rajah, *Sharh 'Ilal* 43 a.
9. Rāzī, *Introd.* 232.

In Arabic literature these words occur: نقد الكلام ونقد الشعر , which mean: He picked out the faults of the language and of the poetry. He separated the good money from the bad.[10] نقد الدراهم

Going through the Qur'ān and *Ḥadīth* we do not find this word used in the sense of criticism. Does this imply that the concept of criticism came very late in *Ḥadīth* literature? No, as a matter of fact, the Qur'ān uses the word *yamīz* for this purpose, meaning "separated one thing from another".[11]

A third century scholar, Imām Muslim, named his book *al-Tamyīz,* whose subject is methodology of *Ḥadīth* criticism. Some *Ḥadīth* scholars used the word *naqad,* but it did not gain currency in their circle. They named the science which deals with criticism of *Hadīth, al-Jarḥ wa al-Ta'dīl* (the knowledge of invalidating and declaring reliable in *Ḥadīth*).

Beginning of Criticism

If criticism is the effort to distinguish between what is right and what is wrong, then we can say that it began in the life of the Prophet. But at this stage, it meant no more than going to the Prophet and verifying something he was reported to have said. Actually, at this stage, it was a process of consolidation so that the hearts of the Muslims might be at ease, as has been described by the Qur'ān in the case of Ibrahim.[12] عليه السلام Dimām b. Tha'labah came to the Prophet صلى الله عليه وسلم and said, "Muhammad, your messenger came to us and told us . . . so and so)" The Prophet said, "He told the truth."[13]

We find this sort of investigation or verifying was carried out by 'Ali[14], Ubai b. Ka'b[15], 'Abdullah b. 'Amr[16], 'Umar[17], Zainab wife of Ibn Mas'ūd[18], and others. In the light of these events, it can be claimed that the investigation of *Ḥadīth* or, in other words, criticism of *Ḥadīth* began in a rudimentary form during the life of the Prophet. This practice of referring to the Prophet ceased naturally with the death of the Messenger of Allah صلى الله عليه وسلم. But it was the duty of Muslim individuals, community and state to follow the way of the Prophet. Consequently they had to be very

---

10. Lane, *Lexicon,* 2836.
11. See, the Qur'ān, *Al-'Imrān,* 179.
12. The Qur'ān, ii, 260.
13. MU. *Imān,* 10, read with BU. 'Ilm 6.
14. Nasā'i, *Sunnan,* v, III.
15. Ḥanbal, v, 143.
16. BU, *Magāzī,* 25.
17. MU. *Musāfirīn,* 120.
18. BU, *Zakāt,* 44.

careful in ascribing statements to the Prophet, and had to scrutinize them carefully.

The first Caliph Abū-Bakr Ṣiddīq, was the pioneer in this field. Next came 'Umar and 'Alī. During this early period there were other Companions too like 'Āisha, and Ibn 'Umar, who carried out criticism of *ḥadīth.*

With the spread of Islām, the *ḥadīth* of the Prophet also began to spread. There were many Companions in the Islamic armies who fought as commanders of entire formations as well as ordinary soldiers in the battlefield. Pious worshippers in the silence of the night and teachers all the time, they were constantly spreading the knowledge of *sunna.* Another factor which helped in disseminating the *ḥadīth* was the concern of 'Umar who used to send teachers of Qur'ān and *sunna* to outlying provinces in good numbers. We know that ten were sent to Basrah alone.[19]

To err is human, so, with the spread of *ḥadīth* in different regions of the Islamic world, the possibility of mistakes arose. Consequently, the necessity for criticism became apparent.

Meanwhile, in the very early stages of the diffusion of *ḥadīth* in the Islamic world, the community faced some very grave events, and there was a great upheaval a quarter century after the death of the Prophet. I refer to the *fitna* of the assassination of 'Uthmān and the war between 'Alī and Mu'āwīya which produced a breech among Muslims. Here, it seems as if the first fabrication of *ḥadīth* began in the political sphere, crediting or discrediting the party concerned. One is quite sure that neither 'Alī nor Mu'āwīya took part in it, nor any other Companion, but there were some who fished in troubled waters and, as the English proverb has it, were more Catholic than the Pope.

At this stage, the general trend in *ḥadīth* learning became more strict. We have already referred to Ibn Sīrīn's statement regarding *isnād.* Regional schools of criticism began to appear. For convenience sake we will deal with two prominent schools of that time, the school of Madīna, and the school of Iraq.

We have just seen that the criticism of *ḥadīth* began in the life of the Prophet. After his death, Abū Bakr, 'Umar, 'Alī, Ibn'Umar, 'Āisha and other companions took part in it. According to Ibn Ḥibbān, after 'Umar and 'Alī came the turn of the Successors Ibn al-Musayib (d.93) ; al-Qāsim b.Muhammad b. Abū Bakr, (d.106) ; Sālim b. 'Abdullah b. 'Umar (d.106) ; 'Alī b. Ḥusain b. 'Alī, (d.93) ; Abū Salamah b. 'Abdur Raḥmān (d.94) ;

19. Dhahabī, *Siyard A'lam al-Nubalā, II,* 345, 363.

'Abdullah b. 'Abdullah b. 'Utbah; Khārijah b. Zaid b. Thābit, (d.100); 'Urwah b. al-Zubair, (d.94); Abū Bakr b. 'Abdur Raḥmān b. al-Ḥarīth (d.94) and Sulaimān b. Yasār (c.100).

It is interesting to note that all of these scholars belong to the first century of *Ḥijra*, though a few of them lived in the first decade of the second century. Later on, in the Madīna region, there were three scholars Zuhrī, Yaḥyā b. Sa'īd, and Hishām b. 'Urwah who learned this science from the above-mentioned scholars. The most famous of these three was Zuhrī (d.124).

In Iraq too the *ḥadīth* critics were active in the first century, prominent among them being Sa'īd b. Jubair, Al-Sha'bī, Ṭāwūs, al-Ḥasan al-Baṣrī (d.110) and Ibn Sīrīn (d.110).

All these Iraqi scholars belong to the first century of the Ḥijra, though some of them lived in the first decade of the second century. After them came the names of Ayyūb al-Sakhtiyānī and Ibn 'Awn. They belong to the first third of the second century.

After this period, the criticism of *ḥadīth* entered a new phase. Though journeying for the acquisition of *ḥadīth* or the *sunna* of the Prophet began in the life of the Prophet, and later on many Companions and Successors travelled a lot, but their journeys cannot be compared to the journeys of scholars during the second and third centuries. The prevailing spirit is described in a saying of Yaḥyā b. Ma'īn (d.233):

"There are four kinds of people who never became mature in their life; among them is he who writes down *ḥadīth* in his own town and never makes a journey for this purpose."

Thus from the second century to a few centuries later a general requirement of a student of *ḥadīth* was to make extensive journeys for learning *ḥadīth*. As the early scholars mostly learned under the scholars of their own locality, their criticism was confined to the same locality. But when people began to learn *ḥadīth* from hundreds and thousands of *Shaikhs* throughout the Islamic world, their criticisms were not confined to scholars of one centre but they began to scrutinize scholars and their *aḥādīth* in general. Due to the extent of these activities, some new centres emerged for this purpose. Let us go back once again to the most famous critics of the second century. Among them were:

Sufyān al-Thaurī of Kūfa, (97-161)
Mālik b. Anas, of al-Madīna (93-179)
Shu'bah of Wāsit, (83-100)
Al-Auzā'ī of Beirut, (88-158)

Ḥammād b. Salamah, of Baṣrah (d.167)
Al-Laith b. Sa'd, of Egypt (d.175)
Ḥammād b. Zaid, of Baṣrah (d.179)
Ibn 'Uyayanah of Mecca (107-198)
'Abdullah b. al-Mubārak of Marw (118-181)
Yahyā b. Sa'īd al-Qaṭṭān, of Basra (d.198)
Wakī' b. al-Jarrāh of Kūfa (d.196)
'Abdur Raḥmān b. Mahdī of Baṣra (d.198) and
Al-Shāfi'ī of Egypt (d.204)

But the most famous one out of them were Shu'bah, Yaḥyā b. Sa'īd and Ibn Mahdī.[20] Shu'ba was the teacher of Yaḥyā al-Qaṭṭān in this field.

The above mentioned scholars in turn produced numerous famous scholars in the field of criticism, but the most gifted ones were:

Yaḥyā b. Ma'īn of Baghdād (d.233)
'Alī b. Al-Madīnī of Baṣra (d.234)
Ibn Ḥanbal of Baghdad (d.241)
Abū Bakr b. Abū Shaibah of Wāsiṭ (d.235)
Ishāq b. Rāhwaih of Marw (d.238)
'Ubaidulah b. 'Umar al-Qawārīrī of Baṣrah (d.235)
Zuhair b. Ḥarb of Baghdad (d.234)

Out of these the earlier three were the most distinguished scholars in this field.[21]

Their most famous students were:

Al-Dhuhalī.
Al-Dārimī.
al-Bukhārī.
Abū Zur'ah al-Rāzī.
Abū Ḥātim al-Rāzī.
Muslim b. al-Ḥajjāj al-Nisāpurī.
Aḥmad b. Shu'aib.

We stop here because this was the most fertile period of *ḥadīth* studies.[22]

Methodology of *Ḥadīth* Criticism

As far as it concerns the criticism of the text or in other words 'documents', there were several methods, but almost all of these methods may be

20. Ibn Ḥibbān, *ibid.*, 16 b.
21. Ibn Ḥibbān, ibid., 17 b.
22. For detail and references of history of criticism, see, Al-Azami, *Intro. to Tamyīz*, 12-18.

brought under the broad heading of 'comparison' or cross question and cross rference. By gathering all the related materials or, say, all the *aḥādīth* concerned, comparing them carefully with each other, one judges the accuracy of the scholars. Ayyūb al-Sakhtiyānī, a Successor, (68-131) says: 'If you wish to know the mistakes of your teacher, then you ought to sit down with others as well.'[23]

Another scholar Ibn al-Mubārak (118-181) says: 'To reach an authentic statement one needs to compare the words of scholars with each other.'[24] Most of the classification of *ḥadīth* was done through this method. The scholars applied it from the very early day of Islam.

The method of comparison was practised in many ways. The following are some of them:

1. Comparison between the *Aḥādīth* of different students of one scholar.
2. Comparison between the statements of a single scholar at different times.
3. Comparison between oral recitation and written documents.
4. Comparison between the *ḥadīth* and the related text of the Qur'ān.

To illustrate the methods I shall give a few examples which should be sufficient.

Criticizing *Ḥadīth* by Comparison Between the *Ḥadīth* of Different Students of One Scholar

For an understanding of the full implication of the method, I begin with the third century scholar Ibn Ma'īn (d.233). He went to 'Affān, a pupil of a great scholar Ḥammād b. Salamah, to read the books of Ḥammād to him. 'Affān asked him whether or not he had read those books to any students of Hammād. Upon which Ibn Ma'īn replied, 'I have read these books to seventeen students of Ḥammād before coming to you. 'Affān said 'By Allah I am not going to read these books to you.' Ibn Ma'īn answered that by spending a few *dirham* he would go to Baṣrah and read there to the students of Ḥammād. He went to Basra to Musā b. Ismā'īl another pupil of Ḥammād. Musā asked him: 'Have you not read these books to anybody else?' He said 'I have read them completely to seventeen students of Ḥammād and you are the eighteenth one.' Musā asked him what he was going to do with all those readings? Ibn Ma'īn replied: 'Ḥammād b. Salamah committed

23. Dārimī, *Sunan*, 1, 152.
24. Khaṭīb, *Jāmi'*, 5a.

mistakes and his students added some more mistakes to his. So I want to distinguish between the mistakes of Ḥammād and those of his students. If I find all the students of Ḥammād committing a certain mistake unanimously, then the source of the mistake is Ḥammād. If I find the majority of Ḥammād's students say something, and some of them go against them then this mistake was committed by that particular student of Ḥammād. In this way I make a distinction between the mistakes of Ḥammād and those of his students.'[25]

Before advancing further, one may comment on this method in a few words: By this method, Ibn Ma'īn not only discovered the mistakes of Ḥammād and those of almost every student of Ḥammād's, but Ibn Ma'īn was also able to grade the different students of Ḥammād and determine their accuracy. This was the most fundamental basis of judgment when *ḥadīth* narrators were graded and put into different categories. This method of Ibn Ma'īn was not invented by him and he was not the first to apply it. We find it in usage from the time of the first Caliph Abū Bakr. There is, of course, a difference in the quantity of the documents concerned, but not the quality, and even this difference was due to dispersal of documents.
Here are a few examples from the very early period.

Abū Bakr and the Comparison of Statements

When a grandmother came to Abū Bakr asking about her share in the inheritance of her grand-son, he replied: "I have not found a share for you in the book of Allah. I knew not that the Prophet has fixed any share for such a case." He asked the Companions about it. Mughīra said that the Prophet gave a grand-mother one-sixth. Upon which Abū Bakr asked him, "Is there anyone with you?" meaning "Can anyone testify to your statement?" Upon which Muḥammad b. Maslamah al-Anṣārī stood up and stated as Mughīra b. Shu'ba had said earlier. Upon this statement, Abū Bakr gave the grand-mother one-sixth. Commenting on this Al-Ḥākim, a great scholar of the fourth century, says that Abū Bakr was the first who took care in accepting the *ḥadīth* of the Prophet. When he heard a *sunna*, he did not base it on the first statement but he had it testified by another.[26]

---

25. Ibn Ḥibbān, *Majruḥīn*, 11 a.
26. See Al-Ḥākim, *Madkhal*, 46. One may think that there is apparently no concordance here between these two statements. But that is not so. When Abū Bakr heard the testimony of Muḥammad b. Maslamah he must have made a comparison between their testimonies to find the agreement and disagreement among them.

'Umar and Comparison

We find that 'Umar, the Second Caliph, applied comparison in several cases.

Abū Mūsā al-Ash'arī went to see 'Umar; He went to the door of 'Umar's home and gave his salutation three times, and getting no response, he returned. 'Umar called him and asked him, what prevented him from entering. He said, "I heard the Prophet saying: 'when one of you asks permission three times and it is not granted, he should go away,' " 'Umar asked him to prove this statement of the Prophet otherwise action would be taken against him. Then Abū Mūsā brought a witness. 'Umar told Abū Mūsā Al-Ash'arī that he did not suspect the authenticity of his statement but he was only concerned that people should be more careful in transmitting the *sunna* of the Prophet.[27]

Abū Hurairah and Comparison

Abū Hurairah transmitted a *ḥadīth* from the Prophet saying: 'He who attends the funeral till the prayer is offered for (the dead), his is the reward of one *Qīrāt,* and he who attends till the dead is buried, for him is the reward of two *Qīrāts'* 'Abdullah b. 'Umar asked him to be careful as to what he transmitted from the Prophet, as he was transmitting too much. Then Abū Hurairah took the hand of Ibn 'Umar and brought him to 'A'isha, who testified to the narration of Abū Hurairah.[28] Later on Ibn 'Umar used to say, "We lost many *qarārīt."* After the companions of the Prophet, the Successors used the same method. A few names may be mentioned in this connection such as Ibn Abū Mulaikah[29], al-Zuhri[30] and Shu'ba etc.

I shall give one example from Muslim, the student of Imām al-Bukhārī.[31] Ibn 'Abbās once spent a night in the room of his aunt Maimuna. After some time—according to his statement—the Prophet stood up, made the ablution, and began to pray. Ibn 'Abbās did the same, and after making the ablution came and stood to the left of the Prophet, upon which the Prophet turned him from the left, and made him stand on his right. This incident was narrated by scholar Yazīd b. Abū Zinād on the authority of

27. Mālik, *Muwaṭṭa, Istidhān,* 3: also, BU. *Buyū',* 9 MU. *Adab,* 36.
28. Ḥanbal ii. 387.
29. Ibn Hanbal, *'Ilal,* 1, 396.
30. BU. *Shahādāt,* 2.
31. MU. *Intr.* 23-4, Rāzī, *Intr.,* 158.

Kuraib, from Ibn 'Abbās, stating that Ibn 'Abbās stood on the right of the Prophet and later on he was made to stand on the left. To explain the mistake of this later statement, Imām Muslim applied the following method.

> He gathered all the statements of the colleagues of Yazīd, the students of Kuraib, who unanimously agreed that Ibn 'Abbās first stood to the left of the Prophet. As a next step, he gathered all the statements of the colleagues of Kuraib and the students of Ibn 'Abbās, who unanimously agreed that Ibn 'Abbas first stood to the left of the Prophet and then was moved to the right. Later on he collected the other incidents where certain companions had prayed with the Prophet when alone. In all these cases it was confirmed that the correct method is that the other man stood to the right of the Prophet. Consequently, he proved that what was related by Yazīd b. Abū Zinād was a mistake.[32]

Example of the Comparisons of the Statement of a Scholar After a Gap of Time

Once 'Ā'isha told her nephew 'Urwah to go to 'Abdullah b. 'Amr and ask him about the *ḥadīth* of the Prophet, as he had learned a lot from the Prophet. 'Urwah met 'Abdullah and asked him about the *ḥadīth* of the Prophet. One of the *ḥadīth* he learned was about how knowledge will be taken away from the earth. 'Urwah returned to 'Ā'isha and narrated what he had learnt. She became discontented about this particular *ḥadīth*. After a year or so, she said to 'Urwah: " 'Abdullah b. 'Amr has come back, go and ask him *aḥādīth* of the Prophet and then ask him the particular *hadīth* concerning knowledge and its removal from earth". 'Urwah went then and asked about the *aḥādīth*. He came back to 'Ā'isha, and told her that 'Abdullah repeated the same *ḥadīth* once again. Upon which she said, "I think he must be correct, as he has not added anything to it and neither has he shortened it."[33]

Comparison Between Written Documents and *Aḥādīth* Transmitted from Memory

Muḥammad b. Muslim and al-Fadl b. 'Abbād were learning *Ḥadīth* in the presence of Abū Zur'ah. Muḥammad transmitted a *ḥadīth* which was not accepted by al-Fadl, and he transmitted it in another way. They argued together, then asked Abū Zur'ah to say who was right. Abū Zur'ah referred

32. Muslim, *Tamyiz*, 136-8.
33. Mu. *'Ilm*, 14.

to a book and found out the said *ḥadīth* where it became clear that Muhammad b. Muslim was mistaken.[34]

A *Ḥadīth* was transmitted by Sufyān through Ibn Mas'ūd, regarding the raising of hands while going for *Rukū'*. Yahyā b. 'Ādam said that he checked the book of 'Abdullah b. Idrīs where he did not find the particular disputed sentence. Commenting on it, Bukhārī says, 'This is correct, because the book is more accurate (*Aḥfaz*) in the eyes of scholars, e.g., a man sometimes narrates a *ḥadīth* and then he goes through the books. In case of difference the version in the book will be accepted as accurate.'[35]

'Abdur Raḥmān b. 'Umar transmitted a *ḥadīth* through Abū Hurairah concerning *Ẓuhr* prayer, which may be delayed in summer from its early time. Abū Zur'ah said that it is incorrect. This *ḥadīth* was transmitted on the authority of Abū Sa'īd. 'Abdur Raḥmān b. 'Umar took it very seriously and did not forget it. When he returned to his town, he checked in his book and found himself mistaken. Then he wrote to Abū Zur'ah, acknowledging his mistake, asking him to take trouble and to inform such and such a person and other people who had asked about it from his students, and to tell them about his mistake, and, he said Allah would give him the reward, for shame is much better than hell.[36]

Comparing the *Ḥadīth* with Related Verses of the Qur'ān

We find that this method was used by 'Umar in rejecting the *ḥadīth* of Fātima bint Qais concerning maintenance money for divorced women.[37] This method was also applied by 'Ā'isha in several cases.[38]

Rational Approach in *Ḥadīth* Criticism

I have described criticism of *ḥadīth* through *isnād* or the chains of narrators. But was pure reasoning or rational approach used in such criticism?

Reason was applied in criticizing *Ḥadīth* at every stage, but strictly speaking, there are limits here to the use of rationalization. The rational faculty helps very little in accepting or discarding the *aḥādīth* of the Prophet. In most of the cases which are dealt with in *ḥadīth* literature, pure reasoning has no place. For example, we find in *ḥadīth* books that the Prophet

34. Rāzī, *Intr.* 337.
35. Bukhārī, *Raf'al-Yadain*, 9.
36. Rāzī, *Introd.* 336, see for another example of referring to the book, *Mizān*, II, 201.
37. Mu. *Ṭalāq*, 46 referring to the Qur'ān, Ṭalāq, i.
38. See Azami, *Introduction to Tamyīz*, p. 48.

used to sleep on his right side, and before retiring to bed he used to recite certain prayers, (*Du'ā*). After getting up, he used to recite certain prayers. He used to drink water in three breaths using the right hand for drinking pots, etc. Now let us check all these statements rationally: A man can sleep on his back, on his right side or on his left side, every position is possible. We cannot say, using our rational faculty, that a certain position is possible and the other is impossible. The same may be said about prayers and drinking water etc.

In all these cases *'Aql* can neither prove nor disprove. What is correct or incorrect can be decided only through reliable eye witnesses and narrators. Thus reasoning itself leads us to accept the statement of honest and reliable narrators, except in cases where we find that the episode goes against *'Aql* (reasoning). From the very beginning, *'Aql* was given its proper place in *ḥadīth* literature. According to al-Mu'allimī al-Yamānī, it was applied at every stage of *ḥadīth*, in the learning of *ḥadīth*, in the teaching of *ḥadīth*, in judging the narrators, and in judging the authenticity of the *ḥadīth*.[39]

Ibn Abī Ḥātim al-Rāzī says: "The goodness of a *Dinār* is known when it is measured against another. Thus if it differs in redness and purity, it will be known that it is a fake. The kind of diamond is examined through measuring with another one. If it differs in sparkle and firmness, it will be known to be glass. The authenticity of a *ḥadīth* is known by its coming from reliable narrators and the statement itself must be worthy of being the statement of Prophethood".[40]

Al-Khaṭīb al-Baghdādī, says: "All the statements come under three categories. Of them is one which is known to be erroneous. The cause of this knowledge is that *'Aql* refused to accept it".[41]

I have tried to give a broad outline of the methodology of *Ḥadīth* criticism, avoiding technical language as far as it was possible. One may say that it is only a glimpse and no more. But I do hope that it will help a non-specialist who wants to know something about the method of criticism. The results produced by this methodology of criticism will be discussed in the next chapter.

---

39. Mu'allimi Yamānī, *Al-Anuwār- al-Kāshifa*, 6-7.
40. Rāzī, *Introduction*, 351.
41. Khatīb, *Kifāyah*, p. 17.

CHAPTER VII

GRADING OF SCHOLARS AND ITS IMPACT ON GRADING OF *AḤĀDĪTH*

The method of criticism which I have discussed helped the scholars in finding out the degree of accuracy of a particular transmitter of *ḥadīth,* resulting in his grading in the light of his literary achievement. However the *Muḥaddithīn* did not consider this sufficient for accepting the transmitted material no matter how accurate the scholars might be.

There were some further requirements which must be met by the transmitter so that his narration may be acceptable.

To accept a *ḥadīth* according to the criteria of *ḥadīth* critics, it is not sufficient that the statement be authentic in itself. Besides this, the narrator must be *'Adl,* i.e. of righteous conduct. In other words his character must be Islamically acceptable.

One of the second century scholars, Ibn al-Mubārak (118-181 A.H., put the problem of personal character in this way. The narrator must be a person who:

Prays in congregation

Does not drink *Nabīdh* (which could cause intoxication if kept for long period of time.)

Does not tell a lie and does not suffer from any mental disqualification.[42] A man may be a great scholar, but if his morals are doubtful, a *ḥadīth* narrated by him is not acceptable.[43] In the opinion of the *ḥadīth* scholars, all the scholars with the exception of the Companions, whose character is testified to by Allah and his Prophet, need this testimony of character if their word is to be accepted. It is obvious, too, that in most of the cases one has to depend on contemporary authorities to find out the personal character of those people. These contemporaries were sometimes influenced by enmity or favor. To deal with such problems, there have been

---

42. Khatīb, *al-Kifāya*, 79.
43. See, Azami, *Studies*, 305.

detailed discussions among scholars, and certain rules have been laid down.[44] In some cases it was and still is possible to discover the falsification and lies, going through historical data, checking the documents, kinds of papers and ink used in the writing. This process was applied by the *Muḥaddithīn,* but it could not be a general method because one cannot always discover the moral integrity of the scholar by this way.

However, when these two faculties; moral character or *'Adl,* and the highest literary accuracy, both combined in a person, he was called *thiqa* (trustworthy), whose narrations are generally accepted by *Muḥaddithīn.*

If a scholar's personal character was acceptable but his literary accuracy was not of the highest grade, and he was the scholar of the second grade, he was called *ṣadūq* (truthful). His narration would be accepted as a genuine one except in a case where he differed from an authority of higher accuracy than him. Next to him comes a scholar whose character was agreeable but his literary achievement was very limited and he committed many mistakes. He was called *ṣadūq yahim.* If a scholar was charged with indecency in his character, material transmitted by him was not accepted no matter how big a scholar he might have been.

Thus to be a man whose transmitted materials are accepted, the narrator must fulfill both requirements: moral and literary. Moral weakness cannot be compensated, though in certain cases literary shortcoming may be overcome.

For example, a man who committed many mistakes in transmitting the *ḥadīth* was called 'weak'. If he narrated a *ḥadīth* alone and no other scholar could verify his narration, then the *ḥadīth* cannot be accepted, for it is suspected of having a mistake in its transmission. But if another scholar though himself a weak narrator in his literary achievement, transmitted a *ḥadīth* which agrees in the meaning and the sense of the early *ḥadīth,* then it would be accepted, though it would be placed in a very low grade, just like a student passing with grade 'D' ('passed').

A system of grading was worked out to place the accepted or rejected statements of scholars. The later scholars have been more refined in grading. Where early scholars have four grades, the later ones have suggested six. Given below are the gradings of Ibn Hajar (773-852) one of the greatest *ḥadīth* scholar of the later period. He placed the scholars in twelve grades.

Ṣaḥābah. The Companions of the Prophet.

---

44. See al-Yamanī, *al-Tankī,* 52-59.

Thiqātun thabt'un. Those scholars who have been awarded the highest marks, such as *thiqatun thabtun,* or *awthaqun-nās,* meaning the most truthful and accurate scholars.

Those who have been awarded good grades without being given superlative degree, such as *thiqatun* (trustworthy) *mutqinun* (accurate) etc.

Those whose position is less than grade three, and have been awarded a good grade, such as *ṣadūq* (truthful).

Those whose grading is lower than No. 4 and given a grade like *ṣadūq yahim.* (truthful, but committing mistakes sometimes)

The one who transmitted a little knowledge, and there is no proof of his being unreliable, nor do we have any positive proof of his high accuracy, is called *maqbūl* (acceptable). If his narration is verified by some other scholars' statements he would be named *layyin* (mild).

One who has more than one student who transmitted *ahādīth* from him, but scholars did not (*tauthīq*) declare him authentic is called *majhūl al-ḥāl* (meaning one whose integrity is not verified), in other words one whose reliability is externally evident, but about whose reliability nothing is known.

One who has not credit from any scholar on his behalf and some of the scholars have spoken against him, is called *d'aīf* (weak).

One who is not known in literary circles at all except through narration of a single scholar, and has not credit of scholars for him is called *majhūl* (unknown).

One who has no certificate of credit at all from the scholars and they have spoken against him giving reasons for their statements, one who committed many mistakes or he was a *fāsiq,* did not meet the legal requirement of righteousness, or was stupid.

One who was charged with or blamed for forgery, is called *muttaham bil kadhib.*

One who was named *Kadhdhāb* (liar) waḍḍā ' (forgerer).

These gradings were mostly followed by later scholars. For every grade there are many terms that have been used by different scholars. Details can be found in Arabic works. Moreover, there is some difference of meaning in the terms used by some of the early scholars. Therefore, a student must be sure in using the grading terms of the early scholars and the standards for which it was used by the particular scholar. For example some universities have the following gradings for the teaching staff: Teacher, Assistant Professor, Professor.

Other universities have the following grading for the same academic purpose and qualifications: Assistant Professor, Associate Professor, Professor.

While these universities agree on the application of the term Professor, they may differ in the application of the term Assistant Professor. The same is true about certain terms used by the early critics in that the meaning and standard of certain terms used by them differ in their implications. Therefore, when one student has insufficient knowledge of these differences, there is every chance that he may make serious mistakes. However, these are the gradings mostly used by the later scholars.

I have explained how the critics were able to grade the literary accuracy and personal character of early scholars, and that they were placed by Ibn Hajar in twelve grades. Their system of grading resulted in the grading of *aḥādīth*.

Grading of *Aḥādīth*

Ḥadīth can be graded into two groups:

Accepted (*maqbūl*) and rejected (*mardūd*)

(1) The accepted ones may be divided into two groups:

Ṣaḥīḥ. (authentic)

Ḥasan. (agreeable)

Both groups are sub-divided into two sub-groups:

Authentic by itself. (*Ṣaḥīḥ li dhātihi*)

Authentic owing to presence of others. (*Ṣaḥīḥ-li ghairhi*)

Ḥasan li dhātihi. (agreeable by itself)

Ḥasan li ghairihi. (agreeable owing to the existence of others)

As a matter of fact this last one is a weak *ḥadīth* which acquires strength from other *aḥādīth* which verify it because the same subject or the same sort of problem dealt with in other *aḥādīth*, which thus support the weaker one.

(2) The rejected ones may be divided into two groups:

Rejected as such, but may be accepted if it acquired strength from outside. However, rejected ones have many names.

Rejected totally.

We shall discuss it later on.

Requirements for *Ḥadīth Ṣaḥiḥ* (Authentic Ḥadīth)

All of its narrators must belong to grades one to three mentioned below:

(1) Continuity of the chain must be preserved, which means the completeness of the chain of transmitters all the way back to the final authority.

(2) Should not be an isolated one, (*Shādh*), which means that particular *hadīth* must not be in contradiction with the narrations of the other authorities who were more in number while belonging to the same group or must not be in disagreement with an authority who has higher reputation than the one under discussion.

(3) Should not have any hidden defect. For example a trustworthy scholar transmitted a *ḥadīth* as being the statement of the Prophet, while majority of the scholar narrated the same *ḥadīth* as the statement of the Companion. Here it becomes clear that this particular scholar committed a mistake in ascribing the statement to the Prophet. But if we do not go into detailed study of the subject and only look to the single chain of the *ḥadīth* it would appear to be the correct one due to the grading of narrators and fulfillment of other conditions. I have mentioned hidden defect, that is called *'illa qādiha,* which implies that the defects are not entirely taken into account. It may be put in the following way:

Usually all the public services require a health certificate of the candidate. Sometimes a candidate looks very handsome and fit for the duty, while the medical examination declares him unfit for the job. In other cases, some of the candidates have a clear defect in their shape or body, but after medical check up they are declared fit for the post, because their apparent defect does not affect the ability of carrying out the duty. The same is true of *'ilal al-hadīth,* illness of *hadīth.* In some cases it affects the authenticity of *ḥadīth* and is called, *'illah al-qādiha,* while in other cases it does not.

***Ḥadīth Ḥasan Lidhātihi* (*Ḥasan* by Itself.)**

All the above mentioned conditions for *ḥadīth ṣaḥīḥ* are required for *ḥadīth ḥasan lidhātihi,* except that any one or all the narrators would be of grade 4, *ṣadūq,* or other terms equal to it.

Ḥadīth Ḥasan Lighairihi

If the narrator of *ḥadīth* belongs to grade 5 or 6 and has some other *aḥādīth* supporting it either in form or in sense only, it would count as *ḥasan li ghairihī.* However, it ought to be remembered that if a chain of *isnād* consists of ten authorities, and nine out of them belong to second grade and only one of them belongs to grade 8, then the *ḥadīth* would be rejected. The overall acceptability is based on the weakest authority. Thus a single weak narrator would result in weakening the *ḥadīth*. If one of the narrators was labeled a liar, and the rest of them were *thiqah* (authentic) and the *ḥadīth* is not known through other channels, then it would be graded as *mauḍū'* (spurious). Even if it has been proved authentic by other *isnād*, the *ḥadīth* would be said to be *mauḍū' bi ḥādhā al-isnād*, 'spurious by this chain'.

It is clear now that in grading the *ḥadīth*, scholars checked the biography of every narrator who took part in transmission of the *ḥadīth*. Later on they verified the narrated *ḥadīth* with other scholars' narrations of the same *ḥadīth* to find confirmation or contradiction, and then they passed their judgment after all possible precautions.

This thorough search for verification gave the scholars ample information about every scholar: how many *ḥadīth* he transmitted, and in how many cases he had other authorities who verified *aḥādīth* transmitted by him, and how many *aḥādīth* were transmitted by him alone and no one shared with him. If a narrator who was graded as *thiqah*, (trustworthy), transmitted some *ahādīth* which were very limited in number compared to the quantity of his transmission, it would be accepted as *ṣaḥīḥ gharīb*, (authentic but strange). But if the narrator was of grade 4 or lower, then it would be graded as *munkar*. However, if the narrator related *ahādīth* frequently which are not in agreement with others either in *isnād* or in the text, then the scholar would be graded as *matrūk*, which means his narrations will not be accepted and *ahādīth* transmitted by him cannot be taken to verify other scholars' *aḥādīth*.[45]

It may come to some minds that in later periods a liar might have fabricated many *aḥādīth* and fabricated first class *isnād* for this sake, and thus was able to circulate those *aḥādīth* as genuine in the circle of *muhaddithīn* who check *isnād* only. But it should be quite clear now that besides checking the data concerning that particular narrator, they would check the same *aḥādīth* to see whether or not they are narrated by other scholars who were the students of the authority mentioned. Thus they would find that the *aḥādīth* are not known except by this narrator, and would label him a liar.

As a matter of fact, the approach of *muḥaddithīn* was very realistic. In our personal experience, if after years of dealing we find someone always

45. See *Mīzān*, iii, 140-1.

correct, then in certain cases we believe his statement even if he has no evidence, unless we have any positive ground on which to falsify his statement. So, after long trial, if we find a narrator accurate in relating hundreds of *aḥādīth,* and he was graded as trustworthy and one who always told the truth then in a case where he has no evidence to support him, we would accept his statement till the contrary is proved.

Rejected *Aḥādīth*

I have discussed the requirements and conditions laid down for accepting any *ḥadīth*. A *ḥadīth* which did not satisfy anyone of these was rejected. However, the causes of rejection may be divided in three groups:

(1.) Rejection owing to defect in narrator. (2.) Weakness owing to discontinuity of *isnād*. (3.) Weaknesses owing to some incidental reasons.

(1) *Rejection owing to defect in narrator*

According to Ibn Ḥajar's grading—as I have mentioned earier—any narrator belonging to grade six or lower than it would cause weakness in *ḥadīth*. However, this weakness would differ. For example if a *ḥadīth* was transmitted by a narrator of 12th grade only it would be called spurious (*mauḍū'*). If he was of 11th grade it would be called *Bāṭil*. If the narrator belonged to grade 10 his *ḥadīth* would be *munkar*. The narrators belonging to these three groups and their narrations cannot be taken as witness to fortify other *aḥādīth*. However, if a narrator belongs to either of the grades from six to eight his *ḥadīth* would be weak, but if he has support of another narrator who belongs to the same grade or to a higher one and narrated *aḥādīth* of the same sense and substance, then this weak *ḥadīth* would be counted as *Ḥasan Li Ghairihi*.

(2) *Weakness owing to discontinuity of isnad*

In this category one may mention, *Mursal, Munqaṭi', Mu'ḍal.* Sometimes *mauqūf* and *maqṭu'* are also mentioned. But as these *aḥādīth* have others than the Prophet as final authority, they are not legally binding.

Mu'an'an also comes in this category if the narrator who used this term was famous for *tadlīs*.[46] In his case it would be counted as a broken chain. But if the narrator was not known for practicing *tadlīs,* and he had learned from the authority from whom he narrated though we do not know that he learned that particular *ḥadīth* from him, or in case we have no positive

46. For the meaning of *tadlīs* see p. 65.

proof of his learning, but there was a possibility of his learning as both lived in one city in one period, then it would be counted as an unbroken *isnād.*

Tadlīs means concealment of defect in goods by merchants who want to sell them. The term is taken from *dalas* which means mixing of light with darkness. This meant a transmitter narrated a *ḥadīth* from an authority whom he met but from whom he did not learn that particular *hadīth* but had learned it from someone else going through that authority. Thus he did not mention the immediate authority and transmitted it from higher authority using a term which can be used for both direct and indirect learning, or used a scholar's name which was not commonly known instead of using the name for which he was famous.

Ibn 'Uyaynah (107-198) is one of the most famous and reliable students of Al-Zuhri (51-124). Once he transmitted a *ḥadīth* saying: *qāla al-Zuhrī*: (Zuhri reported). The students stopped him asking whether he heard that particular *hadīth* from al-Zuhrī? He repeated the same sentence, and was interrupted by the students. He replied: I heard this *ḥadīth* from 'Abdur Razzāq (127-207) who transmitted it on the authority of Ma'mar (96-153) who transmitted it from al-Zuhrī. As Ibn 'Uyayanah was the famous student of al-Zuhrī, he used the word *qāla* (said) which can be used in direct hearing from the authority or through someone else. This is similar to the modern situation when we say that the king or the President said so and so, though we have not opportunity to hear him directly, except through press or TV etc. But this expression may be used in direct hearing as well. Therefore, the one who practised that sort of dubious term was called *mudallis.* Many books have been written on people who committed this sort of discrepancy. Detailed study led to the grading of scholars. They have been put by Al-'Alā'ī in five categories:

a. Those who committed *tadlīs* very rarely and ought not to be placed in this category, such as Yahyā b. Sa'īd al-Ansārī etc.

b. Those who practiced some *tadlīs,* but their narrations were accepted by early scholars for certain reasons such as their fame as great scholars. They were supposed to be aware of the responsibility they were taking on their shoulders by dropping the authority. Or their *tadlīs* was very little in proportion to their total materials. Or they left out the names of trustworthy scholars only.

c. Those who practiced *tadlīs,* were categorized by scholars in various way. Some were counted as people belonging to second group, while other scholars counted them of lower grade and did not accept a *ḥadīth* from them till they explicitly described their direct learning.

d. Those who practiced *tadlīs* and left out even weak and unknown authorities. The chain of their narrations was accepted as unbroken if they explicitly described their direct learning.

e. Those who were weak narrators themselves and practiced *tadlīs*.

The rule is that transmission by those who belong to grades c and d would not be accepted if they did not explicitly say that they learned those *aḥādīth* directly. Transmission by those in grade e was rejected. Narration by those in grades a and b, would be counted an unbroken series even if their terminology does not denote direct learning, except in cases where we have positive information contrary to this. But if a narrator explicitly made a false statement that he learned certain *ḥadīths* from 'certain' authority, then upon being exposed, he would be counted as a liar, and thus all the *aḥādīths* transmitted by him would be rejected.

(3) *Weakness owing to some incidental reasons*

In this category are *Maqlūb, Muḍṭarab* and *Mu'allal aḥādīth*.

(a) *Maqlūb* means upside down. It has been divided in two groups.

i) Reversion in the naming of the authority as it was attributed to someone other than its real transmitter. Thus if it was famous that a *ḥādīth* was narrated by Ibn Dinar from Ibn 'Umar and then someone deleted Ibn Dinar's name and put another name of the same generation, imagining that nobody would transmit this *ḥadīth* by this chain, he would be able to boast that he knew another *isnād* for this *ḥādith* which *is* not known to other scholars. As a result people would learn this particular *hadīth* from him. Those who did this intentionally were called *Sāriq al-ḥadīth.* (Stealer of *ḥadīth.*)

ii) Reversion in the name or in the text by reversing the arrangement, for example: Ka'b b. Murra or Murra b. Ka'b.

(b) *Muḍṭarab* is a *ḥadīth* in which the transmitting authority differed and it was not possible to prefer one narration to another, as both narrators were of equal standard. This defect occurs sometimes in *isnād,* sometimes in *matn,* and sometimes in both. But if it was possible to prefer one narration to another one it would be called *al-Rājiḥ*. For example two trustworthy students of Zuhrī differed in a narration of a *ḥadīth,* but one of them studied under him for a very long period while the other did so for a short period. Here the first one's will be accepted as the correct narration of Zuhrī.

Example of *Mudṭarab:* It is a sin to pass in front of a man who is praying. So while praying it is better to put something in front of oneself as *Sutra,* so that people could pass. But in one *ḥadīth* it occurs that if one does not find anything to put in front, then he should at least draw a line.[47]

The following are some of its *isnād.*

Bishr—Ismā'īl—Abū 'Amr b. Muḥ. b. Ḥuraith—His grandfather—Abū Huraira—Prophet.
Thaurī—Ismā'īl—Abū 'Amr b. Ḥuraith—His father—Abū Ḥuraira—Prophet.
Humaid—Ismā'īl—Abū 'Amr. b. Muḥ. b. 'Amr—grandfather—Ḥuraith b. Salim-Abū Ḥuraira.
Wuhaib—Ismā'īl—Abū 'Amr b. Huraith—grandfather.
Ibn Juraij—Ismā'īl—Huraith b. 'Ammār—grandfather Ḥuraith b. Sulaimān
Ibn 'Uyaynah—Ismā'īl Abū Muḥ. b. 'Amr. b. Ḥuraith—Grandfather.

(c) *Al-Ḥadīth al-Mu'all:* Sick *ḥadīth,* that is usually a *ḥadīth* which apparently seems accurate but has some hidden defect. This defect occurs mostly in *isnād,* as a *ḥadīth* was *mursal* but someone related it as *muttaṣil* or it was a saying of the Companion but in some *ḥadīth* it was attributed to the Prophet.

Sometimes it occurs in the text itself, for example text of two *aḥādīth* got mixed up, or a scholar made a mistake in copying or missed a line in copying. Al-Hākim has divided this defect into ten kinds. There are many books on the subject, perhaps the largest one is *Al-'Ilal* by Daraqutnī, which is still in manuscript form.

We have discussed up till now different kinds of weak *aḥādīth,* that is those which have certain types of shortcomings. The worst of these *aḥādīth* are the spurious ones which were, in fact, falsely attributed to the Prophet. We will, therefore, now deal with this kind of false *ḥadīth* in some detail in a separate chapter.

---

47. See, Suyutī, *Tadrīb,* I, pp. 262-63.

CHAPTER VIII

FABRICATION OF *ḤADĪTH* CAUSES AND MEANS OF ELIMINATION

It is a well known fact that some people are always trying to forge valuable things such as diamonds, jewels, or works of art, etc. For Muslims, except the Qur'an, there was and is nothing more precious than the *sunna* of the Prophet. Therefore, from different motives and for different purposes, different kinds of people fabricated a variety of *aḥādīth*. Some of them were heretics, others were those who had lost their countries to Islam and still others illiterate, though sometimes well-intentioned, Muslims themselves.

The attribution of false statements to the Prophet may be divided into two categories:

(1.) Intentional fabrication of *ḥadīth*. That is usually called *ḥadīth mauḍu'*.

(2.) Unintentional attribution of a false *ḥadīth* to the Prophet by mistake despite due care or due to carelessness. That is usually called *ḥadīth Bāṭil.*

The result in both conditions is the same, that is a statement is falsely attributed to the Prophet. Therefore scholars who collected *aḥādīth* of this sort put them together and did not make separate books for these two types. In many cases, they did not draw a line between *Maudū'* and *Bātil* even in judgment though it would have been useful to know it.

Intentional Fabrication of *Ḥadīth*

1. Those who committed this great sin belong to different categories. Among them were *Zindīqs* who could not fight Islam openly, and took shelter under the cloak of scholarship. The *Zindīqs* included Mughira b. Sa'd al-Kūfi and Muḥammed b. Sa'id al-Shāmī who was crucified for treachery. They imitated the learned scholars, fabricated *aḥādīth* and narrated them to cast doubt in people's minds. Muḥammed b. Sa'īd ash-Shāmī who was crucified reported from Ḥumaid from Anas from the Prophet say-

ing: "I am the seal of the Prophets, there will be no prophet after me unless Allah wills." He forged this exception to support the heresy and infidelity to which he summoned people and to buttress his claim to be a prophet.

However, a very important point ought to be noticed. There were a number of people who were reported to have said that they fabricated certain *aḥādīth* or so many *aḥādīth*..Their claims have been reported without giving any detail of the materials. Sometimes this statement was given by someone who was going to be punished for a certain crime. In some other cases it is attributed to a certain person that after repentance, he confessed that he fabricated so many *aḥādīth*, and he did not know what to do. Early scholars have mentioned their statements without giving any detail. In my opinion, this statement is not sufficient. After confession we grade him as a liar. And it might be a part of a conspiracy that when that person was unable to destroy the faith of the people in the *sunna* of the Prophet, he used this final trick. It is unanimously held that if a man told a lie about the *ḥadīth* of the Prophet, his transmission would not be accepted even after he repented. Therefore, to judge the fabrication of *ḥadīth*, we cannot depend on the statement of a liar.

2. There were some weak-minded people who fabricated *aḥādīth* with good intentions in their mind. Abū 'Umāra al-Marwazī says that Abū 'Isma was asked, "Where did you get from 'Ikrima from Ibn 'Abbās *aḥādīth* about the excellence of the Qur'ān *sūra* by *sūra*, when *'Ikrima's students do not possess this?*" It ought to be noticed how the scholars were making cross references to detect the fault and falsehood. He replied, "I saw that people had turned away from the Qur'ān and occupid themselves with the Fiqh of Abū Hanīfa and the *Maghāzī* of Muḥammad b. Isḥāq, so I forged these *aḥādīth* seeking reward in the next world."

3. There were some story tellers who used to stand in the market places or in the mosques and used to attribute *aḥādīth* falsely to the Prophet.

Scholars mention a class of fabricators who used to fabricate for the sake of rulers. It is very remarkable that one finds only one example of this sort which has been repeated by the scholars.

4. There were certain religious men who fabricated to support their sectarian attitude, either in law or in theology, or in politics or due to their prejudice for race or country or certain people, or those who fabricated for their personal interest. These classes should be put under the category of the people who fabricated intentionally.

Unintentional Fabrication of *Ḥadīth*

There are however, other people who committed mistakes though they did not fabricate the statement itself.

1. Those who took a well known *ḥadīth* and gave it a new *isnād* for the sake of novelty, so that they might become a focus for learning.
2. Those scholars who committed mistakes in transmission, e.g. while *isnād* was ended with the Companion or Successors only, he erroneously attributed statements to the Prophet which were as a matter of fact the sayings of the Companions or Successors.

One ought to bear in mind that as every *ḥadīth* consists of text and *isnād,* and every *isnād* contains many names which usually end with the Prophet, it was quite easy to commit a mistake of this sort where the *isnād* stopped one step earlier.

3. Pious people who did not take the trouble to be exact, and did not give the time and attention required for the study of *ḥadīth,* and were very busy in their *'ibādah* (worship) committed many mistakes in transmitting *aḥādīth.* Yaḥya b. Sa'id al-Qaṭṭān, a second century scholar, reported that "I have not seen more falsehood in anyone than in those who have a reputation for goodness." It implies that the *Muḥaddithīn* were well aware and not impressed by apparent worship and piety.

4. Scholars who learned *aḥādīth* from certain *shaikhs,* and later discovered that there were some other *aḥādīth* transmitted by the same *shaikhs* which they had missed. Instead of being content with what they learnt directly from the authorities or being precise about differentiating what they learnt directly and what they did indirectly, they transmitted all, pretending that they learnt them.

5. Those who learnt books from authorities but did not copy what they learnt at that time. When they grew old and were asked *aḥādīth* by students, their ignorance and desire to appear scholars lead them to transmit *aḥādīth* from copies of the same book which they acquired, but it did not contain notes certifying their learning. It seems that in the 4th century this sort of mistake was common. It ought to be noted that scholars did not allow the transmission of *aḥādīth* from a book, say for example *Ṣaḥīḥ* of Bukhārī, other than the copy which one read to the Shaikh with the chain going back to the author. Then it had to contain a note that a certain student studied it under a certain Shaikh or that the Shaikh permitted him to transmit this book, because it was quite possible that two copies of the same work may differ. There is another opinion, a milder one, that a very

famous book like *Ṣaḥīḥ* of Bukhārī, copies of which were and are very common, may be transmitted if the scholar thinks that the copy in hand, even though it does not contain a note of learning, is similar to one from which he had learnt. However, early scholars did not agree with this, and in some similar cases they labeled the scholar a liar.

6. People lacked the necessary qualifications for teaching of *ḥadīth,* that is a sharp memory, alertness or a correct book. Then a student came and read *aḥādīth* to them which were not transmitted by them but they ignorantly confirmed them. It ought to be noticed that many times students used to do this trick on their teachers to test the knowledge of their teacher. If they found that the teacher was alert and did not fall in their trap they learned from him.

7. Scholars who travelled in search of *ḥadīth* and were recognized *muḥaddithīn,* but lost their books. Later on when they taught students they used copies other than their own, without bearing in mind that there might be some differences between two copies of the same work. Or they transmitted from their defective memories. On this account they resorted to guesswork (*takhmīn*). No doubt the value of what they taught depended on whether their book was sound or not.

Means for Detection of Fabrication in Ḥadīth

Scholars who spent a great deal of their lives with the *aḥādīth* of the Prophet developed a sense which they could use instantly in detecting error. Their example was like that of a man who lived with a beloved friend for scores of years, knew him very well in every situation and so could easily say which statement belonged to him and which not. Similarly a literary critic who studies a poet for a long time and becomes fully acquainted with his style can, on the basis of his perception and personal experience, easily detect a poem which does not belong to the poet. However *Muḥaddithīn* did not depend solely on personal experience as it may be counted a form of subjective criticism. In short if a *ḥadīth* was not transmitted by any trustworthy scholar, and there was a liar or a person accused of lying in the chain of transmission it was said to have been fabricated by that person.

However, scholars laid down certain rules according to which one could reach conclusions about the spuriousness or genuineness of *aḥādīth* even without going into detailed study of *isnād.* Here is a summary of the method described by Ibn al-Qayyim.

Ibn al-Qayyim's description of general rules about rejection of ḥadīth are as follows:

If the *ḥadīth* contains an exaggerated statement that the Prophet could not have made. For example a false *ḥadīth* attributed to the Prophet that when one pronounces *'La ilāha ill Allah'* God creates from this sentence a bird with seventy thousand tongues.

Experiment rejects it.

Ridiculous kind of attribution.

Contradicts a well known *Sunna.*

Attributes a statement to the Prophet which was supposed to have been made in the presence of a thousand Companions but all of them supposedly concealed it.

The statement has no resemblance to other statements of the Prophet.

Sounds like the saying of mystics or medical practitioners.

Contradicts the clear and obvious meanings of the Qur'ān.

Inadequate in its style.

Besides these general rules, the entire system of *isnād* was applied to detect the fabrication.

Scholars had knowledge of almost all the narrators, how many *aḥādīth* they transmitted, how many of these were confirmed by other narrators throughout the Muslim world and how many of them have not been confirmed by other narrators. For this purpose they used the term *La Yutāba'u.*

In many cases even if a *ḥadīth* was well known and authentic but the scholars suspected that a certain narrator who transmitted the *ḥadīth* had not received it through proper channel, they would check the ink and the paper to see whether it was a new writing or an old one.[48]

These are some of the tests which were applied by scholars prior to, or if they did not use it, instead of *isnād* criticism.

Literature on Spurious *Aḥādith*

The early scholars did not merely compile works on spurious *aḥādīth.* They also noted such *aḥādīth* in the books of *'Ilal,* biographies or histories etc. It seems that the first scholar who devoted his book totally to this purpose was Husain b. Ibrāhīm al-Jauzaqānī (d.543). Later on a great number of books were compiled on the subject. The most useful one for a layman is that of Shaukānī called *al-Fawai'd al-Majmū'ah Fi al-Aḥādīth al-Maūdu'ah,* edited by Mu'allimī Yamānī.

48. For detail see, Azami, *Introduction to Tamyiz,* P. 78-9.

Part Two: *Ḥadīth* Literature

1. Earlier Ḥadīth Books: What Happened to Them?

After extensive research it has been found that in the pre-Islamic era some Arabic poetry and some sayings of wise men were recorded. But it is quite safe to assume that the history of Arabic literature begins with the holy Qur'ān, the first book in the Arabic language.

As far as *ḥadīth* literature is concerned, I have established in my doctoral thesis *Studies in Early Ḥadīth literature* that even in the first century of the Hijra many hundred booklets of *hadīth* were in circulation. If we add another hundred years, it would be difficult to enumerate the quantity of booklets and books which were in circulation. Even by the most conservative estimate they were many thousands.[1]

Nature of the Books

The books or booklets which appeared in the first, or even in the early second century, might be put in two categories:

Books containing the *aḥādīth* of the Prophet only, mere collections, without any sort of arrangement of the material.

Booklets containing *aḥādīth* of the Prophet mixed up with legal decisions of the rightly guided Caliphs and other Companions as well as Successors. These materials were also not arranged systematically and formed only some sort of collections.

From the middle of the first century of *Hijra,* books on separate subjects of practical interest began to appear. The booklet of the famous Companion and the Scribe of the Prophet, Zaid b. Thābit (d. 45) on *Farā'iḍ* (share of inheritance) deserves mention here. Later on we find books mentioned by authorities relating to judicial problems such as marriage and divorce, compensation for injuries etc. Thus in the early era when systematic compilation

1. For estimation and detailed study, see, Azami, *Studies in Early Ḥadith Literature,* 34-182.

began the books mixed the *aḥādīth* of the Prophet with the judicial decisions of Muslim authorities and scholars. At this stage it seems that every book was about a single subject.

In the second century the trend changed a little and books covering almost all the legal problems began to appear. The book of Imām Mālik called *al-Muwaṭṭa'* belongs here. It was arranged according to chapters on law covering the whole range of human life, from worship, *zakāt, ḥajj,* marriage, divorce, to agriculture and trade etc. It is a compilation of the *aḥādīth* of the Prophet as well as the opinions of the Companions and Successors.

It is safe to assume that thousands of books in *ḥādīth* literature, which were in circulation in the 2nd century, were not arranged chapterwise. The books which were arranged according to chapters contained a mixture of *aḥādīth* of the Prophet and the sayings and decisions of the Companions and Successors. However, from the end of the second century the literary trend began to change and books containing only the *aḥādīth* of the Prophet with certain systematic arrangement began to appear. Later on in the third and fourth centuries most of the books which appeared contained the *aḥādīth* of the Prophet only. Some books appeared in this period as well which were compiled on the pattern of the second century, such as *Muṣannaf* of 'Abdur Razzāq and Ibn Abū Shaiba (d. 235 A.H.) or *al-Awsaṭ* of Ibn al-Mundir (d.319). However, the bulk of the literature which was produced by the *Muhaddithīn* contained the *ahādīth* of the Prophet only. These books were compiled with different patterns, and were called *musnad, Jāmi', Ṣaḥīḥ, Sunan, mustakhraj,* or *Mu'jam*. Besides the pure *ahādīth* literature hundreds of other books on the subjects relating to *aḥādīth* of the Prophet were compiled. We shall discuss some of the *aḥādīth* books with special reference to one important book of each kind. Some of the books relating to the subjects concerning *ḥadīth* of the Prophet will be listed.

No doubt most of the early books have either been lost or absorbed by the later encyclopedic literature of *ḥadīth,* and thus did not retain their separate entity. But if we understand the literary style of that period correctly we can still locate or rather reproduce many early books. Of course, we may not be entirely sure of their form, but we can produce with certainty the original materials belonging to the early authorities. Let us see the literary style of that period.

What Happened to the Earlier *Ḥadīth* Literature?

I have mentioned earlier that hundreds and thousands of books of *ḥadīth* were in circulation in the first and second century. Only a very small amount of this *ḥadīth* literature has survived. It could be said that either what I have described is totally wrong, or these books were in existence at sometime but were lost later. This second hypothesis raises another problem, i.e. of the negligence of the *hadīth* of the Prophet by Muslim scholars. Is it possible that they did not feel any necessity of *ḥadīth* literature and so it was destroyed?

As a matter of fact, my position is precise and correct. These books were not destroyed nor did they perish, but were absorbed into the work of later authors. When the encyclopedia-type books were produced, scholars did not feel the necessity to keep the early books or booklets, and so, slowly, they disappeared. To explain this point I will describe the method of quotations in early days which would prove my point.

Methodology of Quotations in *Ḥadīth* Literature

No doubt the *ḥadīth* literature at our disposal belongs mostly to the third century. There was a gap of more than two centuries between the authors of these books and the Prophet. What was the level of literary honesty in the learned circle? It is indeed astonishing that they had developed a system of references and of quotations which is unsurpassed even by modern researchers.

The modern method of references and quotations consists of:

Quotations word by word and exact copying put between double quotation marks.

Quoting exactly word by word, but making necessary interpolations enclosed in square brackets.

Quoting exactly but dropping irrelevant details indicating material left out by three dots.

Quoting by paraphrasing, in one's words and expressions.

However, in all these cases one refers to the authorities from whom he quoted, mentioning either books and authors or only one of them.

Muḥaddithīn's Pattern of Quotations

Going through the writing of *Muḥaddithīn,* we find almost a similar pattern of quotations. Here are a few examples.

First method of quotation:

Mālik reported a *ḥadīth* in *Muwaṭṭa'* as follows:

> Mālik from Isḥāq b. 'Abdullah b. Abū Ṭalḥa from Abū Murra, *maulā* of 'Aqīl b. Abū Ṭālib from Abū Wāqid al-Laithī . . .

The same *ḥadīth* is recorded by Bukhari with the same wordings[2], adding an additional authority, Ismā'īl, who reported this on the authority of Mālik.

The same *ḥadīth* is reported by Muslim on the authority of Qutaiba b. Sa'īd who transmitted it on the authority of Mālik with the same wordings.[3]

The same *ḥadīth* is reported by Tirmidhī on the authority of Mālik with the same wordings.[4]

The *hadīth* has been reported several times by Ibn Ḥanbal and other authors as well. Though I have produced it as an example of quotations word by word, it ought to be remembered that in quoting here the book is not referred to at all. Reference is to the authority through whom this information was obtained. Needless to say that the book was used in transmitting this *ḥadīth*.

We may conclude that when certain scholars transmit *aḥādīth* from a certain teacher, and their wordings are very closely similar, it means that in transmitting the information a book was used and memory was not the only basis.

Zuhrī (51-125) compiled a biography of the Prophet which was absorbed into the works of later authors and thus perished in the course of time as a work on its own. Some modern researchers have doubts about this report. Recently almost the whole work of Zuhrī, which is more than 200 pages, has been published in one of the *ḥadīth* works of the third century which has came to light for the first time. Even the editor did not notice that it was the work of Zuhrī. A detailed study was carried out, and it was found that several students of Zuhrī reported portions of this book. This information was recorded by authors who died some 150 years after Zuhrī yet their wordings are very similar, which is almost impossible except if the original book was used.[5]

Second method of quotation:

Quoting exactly word by word, but adding external material in the body of a book.

Most of the people who listened to *aḥādīth* and copied them out had their own books. Students felt at liberty to include additional material even

2. Bukhārī, *'Ilm* 8, *hadīth* No. 66, with the omission of only one word.
3. Muslim, *Ṣaḥīḥ*, *Salām* 26, page 1713, with the omission of only one word.
4. Tirmidhī, *Sunan isti'dhān*, 29, with the omission of only one word.
5. See, Azami, *Introduction to Sīra of Zuhrī*. (Under print).

in a fixed text to clarify some obscure word, or to express their own opinion. As any additional material would have a completely different *isnād* or the name of the inserter, there was no danger of distorting the text.

Examples for this sort of interpolation may be found in almost every book. Here is an example taken from *Ṣaḥīḥ* of Muslim.

> "Qatāda has narrated a *ḥadīth* like this with another chain of transmitters. in the *ḥadīth* transmitted by Jarīr on the authority of Sulaimān, Qatada's further words are: When (the Qurān) is recited (in prayer), you should observe silence, and (the following words are) not found in the *ḥadīth* narrated by anyone except by Abū Kāmil who heard it from Abū 'Awāna (and the words are): Verily Allah vouchsafed through the tongue of the Apostle of Allah (may peace by upon him) this: Allah listens to him who praises Him. Abū Ishāq (a student of Imām Muslim) said: Abū Bakr has (critically) discussed this *ḥadīth*. Imām Muslim said: Whom can you find a more authentic transmitter of *ḥadīth* than Sulaimān? Abū Bakr said to him (Imām Muslim): What about the *ḥadīth* narrated by Abū Huraira i.e. the *hadīth* that when the Qur'ān is recited (in prayer) observe silence? He (Abū Bakr again) said: Then, why have you not included it (in your compilation)? He (Imām Muslim) said: I have not included in this every *ḥadīth* which I deem authentic: I have recorded only such *ahādīth* on which there is an agreement amongst the *Muḥaddithīn* on their being authentic."[6]

This *ḥadīth* has been transmitted by Qatāda with the same chain of transmitters (and the words are): "Allah, the Exalted and the Glorious, commanded it through the tongue of His Apostle; Allah listens to him who praises Him".

Third method of quotation

Quoting exactly, but dropping irrelevant material.

For the third type of quotation we may refer to hundreds of places in *Ṣaḥīḥ* of Bukhārī. It was his habit to cut down *ḥadīth* and quote the portion relevant to the chapter, though he quotes complete *ḥadīth* as well.

For example:

Bukhārī puts the heading of a chapter

"Women's ungratefulness to their husbands, and disbelief is of different grades."

---

6. MU. *Ṣalāt* 63.

Later on he recorded the following *ḥadīth* on the authority of Ibn 'Abbās reporting that the Prophet said: I was shown Hell Fire, and most of its inhabitants were women, as they practise *Kufr*. It was asked: Do they disbelieve (Yakfurna) in Allah? He said (Not for their disbelief in Allah) but for their ingratitude[7] to their husbands and ingratitude to kindness. Even if you were to treat one of them kindly for ever, but if she later saw anything (displeasing) in you, she would say I have never seen any good in you'.[8]

The same *ḥadīth* has been repeated by Bukhārī at least six times in different places. In the chapter of 'Prayer at the time of solar eclipse it is given in full detail, and the portion which has been recorded here appears at the end of that *hadīth*.[9]

Fourth method of quotation

Fourth type of quotation was that of paraphrasing.

It is called in the term of *Muḥaddithīn*: *Riwāya bil Ma'na* which means to transmit a *ḥadīth* using one's own words and expressions. Some of the scholars disapproved of this method while the majority accepted it with the following conditions:

1. The narrator must be a scholar in Arabic language, who knows the words of *ḥadīth* and their full implications and then relates it with some other expression which gives the same sense and meaning though the words were changed. However, it was accepted only in the early days.

After the books were compiled transmission of *ḥadīth* after translation into one's own expression was forbidden.

The early scholars were not fond of paraphrasing. They tried to stick to the words they learned from their teachers, but due to failure of memory they used a synonymous word or an expression equivalent to what they heard.

We have described how the Muslim scholars specially *Muḥaddithīn* in the first century introduced the system of quotations with complete literary honesty. However, there is a fundamental difference between the present day literary style of quotations and theirs. The methodology applied by *Muḥaddithīn* did not allow anyone to quote any *ḥadīth verbally* or from

7. The word *kufr* has two senses, disbelief and ingratitude. The Prophet meant the latter but they thought that he meant the former.
8. BU. *Imān,* 21. For its repetition and dropping of details, see BU. *ḥadīth* No. 431, 748, 1052, 3202 5197.
9. BU. *Khusūf* 9.

any book, except if he had obtained permission from relevant authorities to use it, by one of the recognized methods of learning *ḥadīth*.[10] Thus the terms used in *isnād* such as *Ḥaddathanā* and *Akhbaranā* etc. are a kind of certificate of permission by which a narrator explains how he got this piece of information and is entitled to pass it on to others. But if a scholar has no permission from the authorities, and he obtained the book by buying or copying or as a gift from some unauthorized person and began to quote or transmit *ḥadīth* from it he was named a liar. The scholar must mention that he found it in such and such book but even then the piece of information coming by this way had no value till it is proved by some other means, owing to possibility of a false copy or statements attributed to authorities. The authenticity of most modern documents would be doubtful if the strict criteria of *Muḥaddithīn* were applied to them.

In conclusion, there remains one more point. Under certain conditions the use of one's own expression was permitted and thus there was always a chance of a slight change in the sense. As it is permissible to select only a portion of the *ḥadīth* on condition that it's meaning, sense and impression did not change, there was always a chance that the original document might contain some more information. To make sure of these points constant checks were made through methods called *muṭābi'āt* and *shawāhid*. Thus in case some extra information was found in the narration of a scholar while his colleagues were silent, then if the narrator was of "A" grade this extra information may be accepted, otherwise it would be rejected. This is called *Ziyadāt ath-Thiqah* (extra information from a trustworthy narrator). Meanwhile, if after cross reference it was found that a scholar's paraphrase of a *hadīth* had made its sense wider, it was rejected.

Publishing the Books

The appearance of several editions of the same book with minor alterations, deletion and additions is a common phenomenon in modern times. Similar was the situation in the era of the early scholars various editions of their work contained variations. Let us take the work of Bukhārī on the biographies of *Muḥaddathīn: Al-Tārikh al-Kabīr* which has about 20,000 entries of names with some information about each. The first version was copied by Al-Faḍl b. 'Abbās al-Ṣā'igh. The second version was transmitted by Muḥammad b. Sulaimān b. Faris al-Dallal (d.312). The third and perhaps final version, was transmitted by Muḥammad b. Sahl al-Muqri'. These three versions naturally differ at a few places but the difference is not signifi-

10. See above Chapter III.

cant. Sometimes a student read these different versions to the author. For example Muḥammad b. Ahmad al-Lu'Lu'ī put a note after *ḥadīth* No. 911 in *sunan* Abū Dāwūd that the author did not read this *ḥadīth* in the fourth reading, even though he recorded it.[11] 'Alī b. Ḥasan b. al-'Abd says that he learned Abu Dāwud's *sunan* from him six times. But the sixth time he was not able to complete it. Thus students read in different ways and recorded accordingly. As a result there were differences in versions of the same book. It was easy to recognize when this difference was due to a different student who transmitted the work. But when there was a single transmitter from the author and different students of this *rāwī* or transmitter differed among themselves here and there, putting a heading or discarding it, or mentioning a *ḥadīth* or eluding it, why and how did it happen?

In the case of Lu'lu'ī we have seen how he explicitly admitted that the author did not read *ḥadīth* No. 911 in the fourth reading, yet he put it into the book and transmitted it. He thought that the authors earlier permission to transmit this *ḥadīth* entitled him to do this though the author did not retain it in the later version. Therefore, when a student had a version of a book different from the author's, and he had permission to publish it, then the new version of the book does not cancel the early permission. Therefore this transmitter or *Rāwī*, transmitted a different version of the book to different students causing some variation in this way.

Sometimes mistakes in copying, a word or sentence dropped or a word erroneously used caused this difference. Anyone who has experience of compiling books knows how even after every care some mistakes remain.

Some other problems concerning the methods of early scholars of the problems of authorship and the 'get up' of the books, have been discussed in my work on early *ḥadīth* literature.[12]

Now I shall give brief descriptions of some important authors and their books in hadith literature.

---

11. Abū Dāwūd *Sunan* 1, 331.
12. *Studies in Early Ḥadīth literature*, pp. 200-207.

2. Imām Mālik b. Anas

Mālik b. Anas b. Mālik b. Abu 'Amīr Al-Asbahī. He was probably born in 93 A.H. at Madina though dates ranging all the way from 91 to 97 A.H. have also been given. His grandfather Malik was a Successor and his great grandfather was a Companion of the Prophet. Originally his family belonged to Yeman, and in the time of the Prophet they settled in Madina. His family consisted of his wife Fāṭima and three chilldren: Yaḥyā, Muḥammad and Ḥammād.

It seems that his father carefully looked after his son, and used to revise his lessons with him. Once Malik made a mistake in answer to his father's question, upon which his father told him that this must be owing to the time he spent playing with pigeons. That was a good lesson for Mālik and henceforth he concentrated his full attention on his studies.

He did not travel abroad for learning *aḥādīth* yet had very good opportunity to learn from the famous scholars of the world as most of them visited Madina. The number of his students exceeds a thousand and several books have been written on the subject.

His relations with the political authorities were amicable, though he did not do them any favors. When asked about his relations with the Caliphs and Governors, he replied that they are in need of sincere advice. It is the duty of every learned person to meet them and direct them towards good and forbid them from doing evil.

His Modesty and Far-Sightedness

The Caliph Abū Ja'far asked Mālik to write a book which may be promulgated as the law of the state all over the Islamic world, and it would be used to judge and govern, and anyone who differed from it would be prosecuted. Imām Malik disagreed with this and said that the Companions of the Prophet were scattered all over the Muslim World, especially in the time of the Caliph 'Umar who used to send them as teachers. The people learned from the Companions, and every generation learned from the previous ones. In many cases there is more than one choice in practicing Islam. One of the aspects of Islam has been emphasized by some scholars, while others took other aspects. As a result there has been a variety of methods and most are of equal status. Therefore, if one tries, to change them from what they know to what they do not know they will think it is a heresy. Hence it is better to leave every city with whatever knowledge it has of Islam. Abū Ja'far appreciated this farsightedness.[13] Even when the Caliph wanted that Mālik should read this book to the Princess, the scholar replied. "Knowledge does not go to people but people come to it." When the Caliph requested that other students should not join the class with the Princess, he refused this favor saying they would sit where they found an empty place.

He was physically beaten by order of the Governor of Madina Ja'far b. Sulaimān because one of his *fatwās* (legal decision) was regarded as a move against the authorities. He died in 179 A.H.

His Works

The following works have been attributed to him:

Risālah ilā Ibn Wahb fil Qadr.
Kitāb an-Nujūm.
Risālatun fil Aqḍīya.
Tafsīr Li Ghrīb al-Qur'ān.
Risālah ilā Al-Laith b. Sa'd.
Risālah ilā Abū Ghassān
Kitāb al-Sīyar
Kitāb al-Manāsik.
Kitāb al-Muwaṭṭa'

The fate of most of these books is unknown. However, Mālik is famous for his school of thought, his personal character, his scholarship and his book *Muwaṭṭa'*.

Plan and Purpose of *Muwaṭṭa'*

It records *aḥādīth* of the Prophet and the legal decisions of early scholars of Madina. A famous lawyer 'Abdul 'Azīz b. 'Abdullah al-Majshūn (d.164) compiled a book containing the legal decisions only. Mālik criticised his work and said that if he had compiled the works he would have begun with the *athār* and then followed them with legal decisions. Later on Malik produced his work on this pattern. *Muwaṭṭa'* is not purely a *ḥadīth* book. It contains the *aḥādīth* of the Prophet, legal opinions of the Companions and the Successors and of some later authorities.

13. Rāzī, Int. 29.

He refers very frequently to the unanimous opinions of the scholars of Madina on subjects where there is no *ḥadīth* from the Prophet, or even in understanding the *ḥadīth* of the Prophet and its application.

Quantity of the Material

It seems that he collected a huge amount of material and selected a few thousand *aḥādīth* out of it. Whatever Mālik learned in perhaps forty years is available in *Muwaṭṭà*. He steadily revised this work and as a result reduced the material in it. Therefore, it has more than eighty version. Fifteen of them are more famous and now only one version of Yaḥya b. Yaḥya is available in its original form, complete and printed. This version contains:

Aḥādīth from the Prophet
'Athār from the Companions
'Athār from the later authorities

A vast literature has been produced on this book, and in this context perhaps it stands next to the Ṣaḥīḥ of Bukhārī.

Commentaries on *Muwaṭṭa'*:

The most famous commentaries are by: Ibn 'Abdul Barr who compiled two commentaries. *At-Tamhīd* and *Al-Istidhkār*

Al-Bājī, Sulaimān b. Khalaf (d.474) compiled two commentaries: *Al-Istīfā'* and *Al-Muntaqā,* (mostly an abridgment of the above). Seven volumes.

Az-Zurqānī, Muḥammad b. 'Abdul Bāqī (d. 1122) four volumes printed several times.

Al-Kandhalāwī, Muḥammad Zakarīyā (1315-) wrote *Aujaz-al-Masalik Sharḥ Muwaṭṭā of Imām Mālik,* which has been published more than once in India and Egypt.

3. Aḥmad b. Muḥammad b. Ḥanbal

Abu 'Abdullah Aḥmad b. Muḥammad b. Ḥanbal.

His father Muḥammad was a *Mujāhid* who lived in Baṣra. He went to Marw as a *Ghāzī,* where Aḥmad was born in 20th of Rabī' al-Awwal 164 A.H. Later on, while Aḥmad was still an infant, he was brought to Baghdad. His father died at the age of 30. His mother was Ṣafiyah bint Maimuna bint 'Abdul Malik ash-Shaibānī.

Personal Features

He used to dye his hair, and was a tall, dark brown man.[14] He began to study *Aḥādīth* in 179 A.H. when he was 16 years old and memorized a million *aḥādīth* in his lifetime. He is one of the leading personalities in Islamic history who combined knowledge of *aḥādīth* and law. He was sublime in his God-consciousness and in defending Islam. He challenged the Caliph and his religious authority, was imprisoned for a long time and was treated very harshly by the authorities. But he never surrendered. There are books written on his inquisition.

Ibn Ḥanbal and *Miḥna*

The Mutazilites—so-called free thinkers in Islam—had great impact on the Caliphs Mā'mūn, al-Mu'taṣim and al-Wāthiq who accepted the Mutazilite viewpoint, accepted it as their creed and made it the duty of the state to force it on all Muslims. Ibn Ḥanbal and other *muḥaddithīn* refused to profess it. Ibn Ḥanbal was brought before the inquisition from Baghdad to Ṭarsūs in heavy chains.

Under Mu'tasim he patiently suffered corporal punishment and imprisonment. The Caliph Mu'taṣim requested Ibn Ḥanbal again and again to accept the creed of the Mu'tazilites in which case the Caliph himself would free him of all the chains and follow his steps. After flat refusal Ibn Ḥanbal was trampled under the feet of Mu'taṣim's servants and some of his joints were dislocated. Later a large group of executioners were brought

14. Aḥmad Shākir, *Intro. to Musnad,* 60.

and each of them whipped Aḥmad two stripes with all his strength. After a while Aḥmad lost his consciousness. When he regained consciousness he was offered some drink but refused it saying that he did not want to break his fast. However, this is not the proper place to discuss the suffering of Ibn Ḥanbal for the sake of Islam. A doctoral thesis has been written by Patton on the inquisition of Imām Aḥmad. The most interesting thing in the character of Imām Ahmad is that when the Government's policy was changed in the caliphate of Mutawakkil, in favour of the *Muḥaddithīns'* doctrine, and he was approached to take revenge from those who caused his inquisition, he refused it totally. Imām Aḥmad says that he was going through the meaning of a verse of the Qur'ān (Sūrah Shūrā 40). He found that a great scholar of the first century, Ḥasan al Baṣrī (21-110) explained its meaning saying that in the Hereafter all the nations of the world would be kneeling down in front of Allah. Then it would be proclaimed that those people should stand whose reward is due from Allah, upon which no one would stand except those who pardoned the wrongdoers in this world. Reading this passage Ibn Ḥanbal pardoned his wrongdoers and used to say what does a man lose, if Allah does not punish some one for his sake.

He refused any favor from the Government. Later on, without his knowledge and against his intention some pensions were offered to his sons and cousins. When he came to know of this he almost cut himself off from them. In the early days he used to borrow some things from their houses, but later he refused to have even his medicine and meals to be prepared on their stoves.

His Works

He compiled many works, some of which have been published and some of them have been lost, and some of them still need editing and publishing. Here is a list of some of his works:

Al-'Ilal wa Ma'rifat ar-Rijāl
Tārikh
An-Nāsikh wal-Mansukh
At-Tafsīr
Al-Mānasikh
Al-Ashribah
Az-Zuhd
Ar radd 'Ala az-Zanādiqa wa al-Jahmīya
Al-Musnad

Of all of his works, he is most famous for *Musnad.*

Nature of *Musnad* Works

Musnad works are not compiled in accordance with issues in Law. The only criteria is to collect *aḥādīth* of a certain companion in one place. However, the compilers differ in arrangements of the names of the companions. Some of them begin with the four righteous Caliphs Abu Bakr, 'Umar, 'Uthmān and 'Alī, followed by the remaining six of them who had tidings of Paradise from the Prophet. These are followed by the Companions who embraced Islam first, and so on. Some of the books are arranged alphabetically and some according to regions. However, the *Musnad* is not easy to use because there is no subject by subject arrangement of material at all. Thus it is very difficult to find a particular *ḥadīth*.

Musnad was published in six volumes in 1313 A.H. A number of books have been compiled on the *Musnad* of Imām Aḥmad. In this century two scholars contributed the best part of their lives in the service of this book. One was Shaikh Aḥmad 'Abdur Raḥmān as-Sā'ātī father of Imām Ḥasan al-Bannā, founder of the famous Society of Muslim Brothers, who arranged the original work according to chapters on legal matters. It has a good commentary and references to relative *aḥādīth* in other works. The book has been published in 24 volumes and is one of the best works on *Musnad*. The other scholar was Aḥmad Shākir who intended to publish a critical edition of the work in its original form. He published about a quarter of the original work in 15 volumes before he died. However, up till now its *aḥādīth* have not been counted. Scholars estimate that there are between 30,000-40,000 *aḥādīth*. This is perhaps the biggest book on *ḥadīth* at the present in our hands, or it might be the second biggest work. There have been many other works on *ḥadīth* much larger than *Musnad* of Imām Aḥmad but these are no longer extant. However, over 80 *Musnads* have been mentioned by Kattānī in his book *ar-Risālah al-Mustaṭrafah* (p. 74), some of them very voluminous. Ya'qūb b. Shaiba made a plan to compile a *musnad* work. If he had been able to complete it this huge project would have exceeded 200 volumes. A tiny part of this grand book was discovered and has been published. A partial list of Musnads is given below:

Musnads by (1) 'Abd b. Ḥumaid (2) Abū Ishāq (3) Abū Ya'lā (d.307) (4) Al-Bazzār (d.292) (5) Ḥasan b. Sufyān (6) Ḥumaidī d.2) (7) Ishāq b. Rāhwaih (8) Ṭayālisī (9) Usāma b.Ḥārith (10) Ya'qūb, b. Shaibah (d.262)

4. Imam Bukhārī

Abū 'Abdullah Muḥammad b. Ismā'il b. Ibrāhīm b. al-Mughira al-Ja'faī was born on Friday 13th Shawwāl 194 A.H. at Bukhārā. His father Ismā'īl was a scholar of *ḥadīth,* who studied the subject under some very famous scholars such as Mālik b. Anas, Ḥammād b. Zaid and Ibn al-Mubārak. While Bukhārī was quite young his father died. Bukhārī inherited a good fortune from his father. He entrusted it to someone for partnership. One of the clients owed him 25,000 dirhams and did not intend to pay it. It was suggested that Bukhārī should take the case to the Governor so as to obtain the amount, but he refused to take any help from the Governor, thinking that the Governor might later ask him for favors. Bukhārī had an affectionate mother and an older brother named Aḥmad.

Bukhārī began the study of *Ḥadīth* while he was quite young, even less than ten years of age. By the age of sixteen, he had memorized many books of prominent early scholars such as Ibn al-Mubārak, Wakī' etc. He did not content himself with memorizing *aḥādīth* and books of early scholars, but also learned the biography of all the narrators who took part in transmission of any *ḥadīth,* their date of birth, death, place of birth and so on.

He stayed in Ḥijaz for six years to learn *ḥadīth.* He journeyed to Baghdad eight times. In one of his journeys to 'Ādam b. Abū Ayās his money was finished. Penniless, he lived for a time on the leaves of wild plants. He was an excellent marksman and used to go outside for practice that he may be ready for *Jihād* all the time.

In criticizing the early scholars to evaluate them he used very moderate and mild language but scholars know very well what those soft words of Bukhārī meant. He was very generous to his students. His scribe Muhammad b. Abū Ḥātim says: "Bukhārī used to wake up in the night dozens of times, lit the lamp by flint, made some marks on certain *ḥadīth* and then slept. I asked him: "Why did you not call me and you suffer all these things alone." He replied: "You are young and I did not wish to disturb your sleep".

When Bukhārī arrived in Baghdād, scholars gathered to examine his famous memory. They appointed ten men, everyone of them to read ten *aḥādīth*. All of them changed the *isnād* and put it with different *matn*. One by one they began to read *aḥādīth* asking him whether he knew it. He constantly replied, "Not known to me". Those who knew that it was an actual examination of Bukhārī said that he understood the case, while the general impression was that Bukhārī's knowledge was very meagre and his memory was very bad. After the questions ended, he systematically explained to them which *isnād* belonged to which *ḥadīth*.

In his last days he faced some hardship and was ordered by the governor to leave the country. I do not know whether it was the curse or blessing of Bukhārī that the name of the governor has become part of history whereas hundreds of kings have been forgotten.

Bukhārī died on Saturday, night of 'īd in 256 A.H.

His Works

Bukhārī compiled many works, some of them perished while others are in our hands.

1. *Qaḍāyā as-Ṣahabah wat-Tābi'īns*
   He compiled it when he was eighteen, and at present no information is available about it.
2. *Raf'al-Yadain*
3. *Qirā'at khalf al-Imām*
4. *Khalq Af'āl Al-'Ibād*
5. *at-Tafsīr al-Kabīr*
6. *Al-Musnad al-Kabīr*
7. *Tārīkh Ṣaghīr*
8. *Tārīkh Awsaṭ*
9. *Tārīkh Kabīr* (8 vols.)
10. *al-Adab al-Mufrad*
11. *Birr al-wālidain*
12. *Aḍ-ḍu'afā'*
13. *Al-Jāmi' al-Kabīr*
14. *Al-Ashriba*
15. *Al-Hibah*
16. *Asāmī aṣ-Ṣaḥāba*
17. *Al-Wuḥdān*
18. *Al-Mabṣut*

19. *Al-'Ilal'*
20. *Al-Kunā*
21. *Al-Fawā'id*
22. *Ṣaḥīḥ of Bukhārī.*

Books No. 2, 3, 4, 7, 9, 10, 12 and 20 have been published, some of them several times. However, his most famous work is *Ṣaḥīḥ of Bukhārī*. Its full title is *Al-Jāmi' al-musnad Aṣ-ṣaḥīḥ al-Mukhtaṣar min umūr Rasulillāhi wa sunanihi wa Ayyāmihi,* which means: An epitome containing all types of authentic *musnad aḥādīth* concerning the Prophet, his *sunna* and his wars. He spent sixteen years in its compilation. It seems that he made the framework for his book while he was in Makka in the *Masjid al-Ḥarām*. He worked on it continuously and the final draft was made in the Masjid of the Prophet.

For every *ḥadīth* he selected to put in his *Ṣaḥīḥ,* Bukhārī used to take a bath and pray two *rák'ah nafl* and made *istikhāra*. Later on, if he was satisfied he put the *ḥadīth* in his book.

Number of *Aḥadith* in Ṣaḥiḥ of Bukhari

Bukhārī habitually took a portion of the *ḥadīth* for the heading of the chapter. Also he repeated *aḥādīth* time after time according to their legal deductions. The number of *aḥādīth* in his book is 9,082 but without repetition it goes down to 2,602. This number does not include *aḥādīth mauqūfah* and sayings of successors.

His Methods of Revision

Usually authors make changes in their works and bring out new editions improving on the earlier one. So did al-Bukhari. He stated that he composed his work thrice. We know for sure that his *Tārikh Kabīr* was published three times and every edition differs a little and the last one was the most accurate. He did the same with his *Ṣaḥīḥ*. Even after this final draft he continually made changes in it, adding and discarding, sometimes putting new headings, even without filling in the material required for them.

His Conditions for Acceptance of *Ḥadīth* for his Ṣaḥiḥ

He laid down the most strict conditions.

The narrator must be of a very high grade of personal character, of a very high grade of literary and academic standard.

There must be positive information about narrators that they met one another and the student learned from his Shaikh.

It is as difficult to obtain complete data about every scholar. In fact we do not have complete information about any scholar's list of students. There was a difference of opinion relating to this matter between Bukhārī and Muslim. In Muslim's opinion if two scholars lived together where it was possible for them to learn from each other, then, even if we have no positive information about their meetings, we should accept their *aḥādīth,* regarding their *isnād* unbroken provided that they were not practicing *Tadlīs.* Bukhārī did not agree with this position. He insisted on positive evidence of learning and teaching. He did not consider even this condition sufficient and required further scrutiny in selecting authorities.

Criteria in Selecting the Material

Most of the authors of six principal books of *ḥadīth* did not describe their criteria in selecting the material, except for a sentence here and there, but it is possible to arrive at some conclusions from their writings. Two scholars of the sixth century, Ḥāzimī and Maqdisī studied the subject. They studied the qualities of narrators whose *aḥādīth* have been recorded in those books and tried to find out a general rule. Ḥāzimī says that those scholars had certain criteria in accepting a narrator whose *ḥadīth* they were going to record in their books. For example one who wishes to record only authentic *aḥādīth* must be careful of the narrator and his teacher and their positions. Sometimes a certain narrator is a very good and accurate narrator from one teacher (shaikh) while he committed mistakes in narrating from another one. It means that in the first case his *aḥādīth* would be accepted while in the second case it would be rejected. If we take the comparable example of students, it seems that certain students obtain good results when they study the subject under certain professors. But the same students get poor marks either in another subject or in the same subject if they study under certain other professors. Meanwhile there are students who get 'A' in every subject whoever their teacher might be. This fact was observed by early scholars. To explain it more simply Ḥāzimī takes the example of Zuhrī who had a great many students. Ḥazīmī divided them in five categories:

1. Narrators from Zuhrī who possessed the high quality of *itqān'* accuracy, *Ḥifẓ,* (excellent memory) and a lengthy companionship with Zuhrī, accompanying him even in his journeys.

2. The second group was *'adl* like the first group but they did not spend sufficient time with Zuhrī to be able to remember his *hadīth* thoroughly and with accuracy, and thus were placed a little below group 1.
3. Those who lived long with Zuhrī like the first group but have been criticized by the scholars.
4. Those who have been criticized by the scholars and meanwhile did not spend much time in the lectures of Zuhrī.
5. Those who are held as weak narrators, or not known to early scholars.

In his *Ṣaḥīḥ,* Imām Bukhārī mostly recorded the *aḥādīth* narrated by the first group, but sometimes recorded the *aḥādīth* of the second group as well.

Imām Muslim sometimes recorded the *aḥādīth* of the famous scholars of the third group as well. However, Nasa'ī and Abū Dāwūd quote frequently from the first, second and third groups. Abū Dāwūd sometimes mentions *aḥādīth* of the fourth group as well. Tirmidhī records *aḥādīth* of the first, second, third and the fourth group, but he describes the weak narrators, a method not generally applied by Nasa'ī or Abu Dāwud.

However, it is obvious that not all the scholars were famous like Zuhrī, nor did all of them have so many students. Therefore, the rule which I have mentioned now regarding the group of the students of a certain scholar is applicable only to famous scholars who had many students.

In case of a scholar who had a few students, Bukhārī and Muslim accepted the material on the basis of trustworthiness and accuracy. Therebefore, they sometimes recorded a *ḥadīth* even if the narrator had no other fellow who transmitted the same *aḥādīth,* as they were sure about the accuracy of that narrator due to their examination in other matters, but in most of the cases they recorded the *aḥādīth* of trustworthy persons which was attested to by other students' witness.[15]

Translation of Ṣaḥiḥ

The book has been translated into many languages, completely or partially.

Exegeses of *Ṣaḥiḥ:*

Hundreds of exegeses have been written on the book, some of them exceeding 25 volumes.

---

15. Ibn Ḥajar, *Hady as-Sāri,* I, 6.

The best ones are:
Fatḥul Bārī by Ibn *Ḥajar* (d.852) is the best one available.
'Umdatul Qārī by 'Ainī (d.855).
Irshād as-Sāir by Qasṭallānī (d.923)

Criticism of Bukhari

Many scholars criticized Bukhārī's work. The criticism concerns about 80 narrators and some 110 *aḥādīth*.[16] The criticism showed that though these *ahādīth* were not mistaken or false they did not measure up to the high standard which was set by Bukhārī.

A comparable example would be that of some colleges which do not accept any student less than 'A' grade, but after scrutinizing it may be found that they accepted in the mass of the students a few students of lower grade, say of grade 'C'. This criticism implies that the highest grade was given to Bukhārī after very severe test. But it seems that in accepting the narrations of those low grade scholars he had some other evidence which satisfied him about the correctness of the *ahādīth* he accepted.

Trimidhī, speaking about Ibn Abi Laila says:

قال احمد : لا يحتج بحديث ابن أبي ليلى،وقال محمد بن اسماعيل:
ابن أبي ليلى هو صدوق ولا أروى عنه لأنه لا يدرى صحيح حديثه من
سقيمه وكل كان مثل هذا فلا أروى عنه شيئاً.

"Muḥammad b. Ismā'īl (al-Bukhārī) said: "Ibn Abī Lailā is truthful صدوق but I do not transmit any *ḥadīth* through him, as it is not known which of his *ahādīth* are correct, which erroneous. And anyone who was of this kind I do not relate *ḥadīth* through him".[17] It means that even a scholar of this grade was not acceptable to Bukhārī, except if he finds some means to differentiate among his *aḥādīth*. For example if he had old copies or original of the teachers of Ibn Abī Lailā, and which was later transmitted by him Bukhārī would accept those *aḥādīth*, because he would be sure that Ibn Abī Lailā did not commit a mistake in transmission of these *aḥādīth*.

May Allah reward all of them as well as us.

Other Books called Ṣaḥiḥ

Beside Bukhārī, there are several books called *Sahīh* such as:
Ṣaḥīḥ of Ibn Khazaima

---

16. Suyuṭī, *Tadrīb*, I, 134; Ibn Ḥajar, Hady as-Sārī, II, 106.
17. Tirmidhī, *Sunan*, II, 199.

Ṣaḥīḥ of Ibn Ḥibbān

Ṣaḥīḥ of Ibn as-Sakan (d. 353)

Ṣaḥīḥ of ash-Sharqī, a student of Imām Muslim, died in 325 A.H. But the most famous one after Bukhārī is *Ṣaḥīḥ* of Imām Muslim which deserves some detailed study.

5. Abul Ḥusain Muslim b. al-Ḥajjāj al-Nisāpuri

He was born in 204 A.H. Unfortunately, available sources do not give us information regarding his ancestors, family and his early childhood. No doubt, he must have studied the Qur'ān, Arabic literature and grammar, before beginning the study of *ḥadīth* as it was the pattern of that period. However, he began the study of *ḥadīth* in 218 A.H. at the age of about 15 years.

As *riḥla* (journey) for the study of *ḥadīth* was an essential element, Imām Muslim visited almost all the centres of learning many times. Perhaps his first journey was to Makka for Hajj in 220 and in this journey learned from Qa'nabi and others, then he returned to his homeland in short time. It seems that his real *riḥla* began about 230 A.H. He journeyed to Iraq, Ḥijāz, Syria and Egypt. The last time he went to Baghdad was in 259 A.H.

His Teachers

The biographical works have mentioned a good deal of his teachers' names. We may mention a few of them, such as Zuhair b. Ḥarb, Sa'īd b. Manṣūr, 'Abd b. Humaid, Dhuhalī, Al-Bukhārī, Ibn Ma'īn, Ibn Abī Shaiba etc. However, their numbers are in hundreds.

His Students

The number of his students is very large. Hundreds of people read his books to him. We may mention a few of them, such as Tirmidhī, Ibn Abū Ḥātim Rāzi, Ibn Khuzaimah etc.

His Generosity

He was a merchant of good fortune and of best reputation. Dhahabi called him محسن نيسابور.[18]

---

18. *Dhahabī, 'Ibar,* II, 231.

Muslim and Bukhari

Muslim benefitted from *Ṣaḥīḥ* of Bukhārī and later compiled his own work, and was was influenced by Bukhārī's method. When Bukhārī came to Nisāpur, Muslim attended to him and used to visit him. Ahmad b. 'Abduh describes one of the meetings of Muslim and Bukhārī, saying: Muslim came to Bukhārī and kissed him on his forehead, and said, "Let me kiss your feet, O Master of *muḥaddithīn* and Doctor *of Ḥadīth.*"

There was a difference of opinion in theological questions between Bukhārī and Dhuhalī, upon which Dhuhalī asked his students not to attend the lectures of Bukhārī and most of them obeyed. Later Dhuhalī was informed that Muslim still visited Bukhārī. Dhuhalī declared anyone who followed Bukhārī's opinion should stay away from his lecture. Though he did not mention Muslim explicitly, yet Muslim understood it, and went to the house, and sent back with a porter all the books which he had written earlier from the lectures of Dhuhalī.

His Works

He compiled many books such as:

1. *Al-Asmā'wa al-Kunā.*
2. *Ifrād ash-Shāmiyīn*
3. *Al-Aqrān.*
4. *Al-Intifā' bi Julūd as Sibā'.*
5. *Aulād as-Ṣaḥābah.*
6. *Awhām al-Muḥaddithīn.*
7. *Al-Tārikh*
8. *At-Tamyīz*
9. *Al-Jāmi'*
10. *Ḥadīth 'Amr b. Shu'aib*
11. *Rijāl 'Urwah*
12. *Sawālātuh Aḥmad b. Ḥanbal*
13. *Ṭabaqāt*
14. *Al-'Ilal*
15. *Al-Mukhadramīn*
16. *Al-Musnad al-Kabīr*
17. *Mashā'ikh ath-Thaurī*
18. *Mushā'ikh Shu'bah*
19. *Masha'ikh Mālik*
20. *Al-wuḥdān*
21. *As-Ṣaḥīḥ al-Masnad*

According to the report of Ibrāhīm b. Muhammad b. Sufyān, Imām Muslim compiled three books of *Musnadāt*:

1. Which he read to the people that is *Ṣaḥīḥ*.
2. Which contain *aḥādīth* of even some weak narrators.
3. Which contain even the weak narrators.[19]

Numbers 8, 20 and 21 have been published.

Numbers 1, 11, 13 are still in manuscripts in different libraries.

However, his most important work is *Ṣaḥīḥ,* which is the short form of the title. The original title is as following: *al-Musnad as-Ṣaḥīḥ, al-Mukhtaṣar min as-Sunnan, bi naql al-'adl'an al-a'dl 'an Rasul Allah.* [20]

Nature of This Work

He did not pay any attention to legal extraction. He did not even mention the chapters which were added later.

Utmost attention was paid for *mutāba'āt* and *shawāhid.*

This book comes next to the *Ṣaḥīḥ* of Bukhārī and a vast literature has been produced around this book. It seems that Muslim presented his book *Ṣaḥīḥ* to Abū Zur'ah, one of the greatest critics of *ahādīth,* and wherever Abū Zur'ah pointed out any defect in any *ḥadīth,* Muslim omitted it without argumentation. Because he did not want to record *ṣaḥīḥ aḥādīth* according to his own criteria alone, he recorded only those whose authenticity was accepted among scholars. This is clear from his own statements in the *Ṣaḥīḥ* that he recorded only what was unanimously accepted as authentic.[21]

Number of *Aḥādīth* in *Ṣaḥīḥ* Muslim

According to the numbering of Muḥammad Fuwād 'Abdul Bāqī of *Ṣaḥīḥ* Muslim, it contains 3033 *aḥādīth.* His method of numbering is not based on *isnād* system. He based his counting on subjects. We know *Muḥaddithīn* usually count by *isnād.* Therefore, if we apply their method, the number would increase perhaps to double.

Exegeses or Commentaries

There are many commentaries on this book. The most popular and widely used one is that of Imām an-Nawawī, (d.676) called *Al-Minhāj fī Sharh Ṣaḥīḥ Muslim b. Al-Ḥajjāj.* This commentary has been published several times.

19. Ibn Khair, *Fihrist* 102.
20. Ibn Khair, *Ibid.*, 98.
21. MU. *Salāt* 63.

6. Abū 'Abdur Raḥmān Aḥmad b. Shu'aib b. 'Alī b. Sinān b. Baḥr al-Khurāsānī an-Anasa'ī.

He was born in 215 A.H. He took extensive journey to learn *aḥādīth* of the Prophet. He started travelling for this purpose when he was 15 years old. He learnt *aḥādīth* in Khurasan, Iraq, Arabia, Syria, Egypt and al-Jazīra etc. He was a great scholar and critic. Some of the later scholars even esteemed him higher than Imām Muslim in his knowledge of *aḥādīth*. He went for *jihād* accompanying the Governor of Egypt. He was very brave, and in the military camp he used to try to guide the Governor and army to teach them *sunna* of the Prophet and asked them to follow it. Meanwhile, he did not attach himself to the company of the governor. He lived in Egypt for a long time. We know about his son 'Abdul Karīm, himself a *muḥaddith*, and a narrator of *sunan mujtabā* who died in Egypt in 344 A.H.[22]

He was selective in his material, and did not use some very important material because of one of the narrators Ibn Lahī'ah was labeled as a weak narrator, because Ibn Lahī'ah's books were burnt he had to depend on other scholars' copies of the same work. But as these copies did not bear the name of Ibn Lahi'ah in reading certificate, therefore Ibn Lahi'ah was supposed not to transmit any *ḥadīth* from those books.

Nasa'ī was very accurate in his recording. There was some misunderstanding between him and his teacher Al-Hārith b. Miskīn. Therefore Nasa'ī did not participate in the circle of Al-Hārith but used to sit somewhere from where he could learn what was taught without being seen. When recording those *aḥādīth* Nasa'ī used to write: I heard this *ḥadīth* while it was read to al-Hārith bin Miskīn.

His Works

He compiled many works, some of which were:
As-Sunan al Kubrā
As-Sunan al-Mujtabā

---

22. Ibn Khair, *al-Firhrist*, 117.

Kitab at-Tamyīz
Kitab aḍ-ḍu'afā'
Khaṣā'is 'Alī
Musnad 'Alī
Musnad Mālik
Manāsik al-Ḥajj
Tafsīr

It is quite possible that some of the above mentioned books may be the part of *as-Sunnan al-kubrā.*

Sunan of Nasa'ī

However, his most famous work is *As-Sunan al-Mujtabā,* which is, as a matter of fact, selection from *as-Sunan al-Kubrā* with some editions. It is said that when he compiled his great book *as-Sunan al Kubrā,* presented it to the Governor of Ramlah, the Governor asked him whether or not all the *aḥādīth* recorded into it are authentic, Nasa'ī replied in the negative. The Governor asked him to select only authentic ones, thus by this way *Mujtabā* was compiled. But Nasa'ī did not content himself even in this book with authentic *aḥādīth* only. He recorded even weak *aḥādīth* as well. Thus, it seems that the story of the Governor is of doubtful nature.

Actually it is a part of his methodology. He tries to record the different *isnāds* of *aḥādīth,* then records the *isnād* where some mistakes have been committed by narrators, then explains what is correct.[23] Thus he recorded the weak *aḥādīth* as well, but mostly to show what defect they had.

It was assumed for a long time that *as-Sunan al-Kubrā* has been lost, but الحمدلله lately it has been discovered in Turkey and half of it is in Mau, my home town in India.

Commentaries on *Sunan* of Nasa'ī

In this regard the book of Nasa'ī did not attract the attention of early scholars. Much later Suyuṭī wrote a short commentary on the book, titled: *Zahrur Rabā 'Ala Al-Mujtabā,* which has been published several times.

Nasa'ī died in 303 A.H. However, there is difference among scholars about the cause as well as the place of his death.

---

23. Ibn Rajab, *Sharh 'Ilal,* 15 b.

7. Abū Dawūd Sulaimān b. al-Aash'ath Al-Azdi as-Sijistanī

He was born in 202 A.H. He must have studied the Qur'ān, Arabic literature and some other subjects as it was the custom of the time before beginning the study of *ḥadīth.* He travelled extensively for the study of *ḥadīth.* It is reported that he journeyed to Khurasān, Rayy, Harāt, Kūfā, Baghdād, Tarsūs, Damascus, Egypt and Basra. We find him in Baghdād in 221 A.H. It means that he started his journey for the learning of *aḥādīth* while he was less than 20 years old. He spent 20 years in Ṭarsūs.

He gained a wide reputation in his lifetime. Baṣrā was deserted due to disturbance of Zanj in 257 A.H. The Governor Abū Aḥmad visited Abū Dāwūd in his house in Baghdād and requested that he move to Basrā so that the deserted city may be rehabilitated by his presence and gathering of the scholars and students.

The scholars are unanimous about his great ability, trustworthiness, honesty and accuracy. He was not only a narrator of *aḥādīth* and a good collector and compiler, but also a good lawyer and a very good critic. It is interesting to read that while criticizing the *aḥādīth,* he sometimes checked the written material, papers, and ink to discover their age. He criticized his own son 'Abdullah, denouncing him as a liar.

His Family

He was married and had children. One of his teenaged sons used to go with him to study in the circle of *ḥadīth* scholars.

Abu Dāwud died on Friday, 15th Shawwāl, 275 in Baṣra.

His Works

Al-Marāsīl

Masā'il al-Imām Aḥmad

An-Nāsikh wal-Mansūkh

Risālah fī waṣf kitāb as sunan

Az-Zuhd

Ijābāt'an Sawalat Al-'Ājurrī

As'ilah 'an Aḥmad b. Ḥanbal
Tasmiyat al-Akhwān
K.al-Qadr
Al-Ba'th wan-Nushūr
Al-Masā'il allati halafa 'alaihā al-Imām Ahmad
Dalā'il an-Nubūwāt
Faḍā'il al-Anṣār
Musnad Mālik
Ad-Du'ā'
Ibtidā' al-waḥy
At-Tafarrud fis sunan
Akhbār al-Khawārij
A'lām an-Nubuwāt[24]
Sunan

Nature of *Sunan* Books

We have seen earlier the meaning of *sunna,* (plural *sunan*) but when the authors of *ḥadīth* books titled their books *sunan,* they meant that the book had been chapterized according to legal chapter such as *Ṭahāra, ṣalāt, zakāt* etc. related on the authority of the Prophet, and the opinions of the companions are usually not mentioned in it.

Therefore these *sunan* books do not contain the *aḥādīth* concerning morality, history, and *zuhd* etc.

Sunan of Abū Dawūd

It seems that he compiled his book *Sunan* while he stayed in Ṭarsus for twenty years. He selected some four thousand eight hundred *aḥādīth* from 500,000 for this purpose. He was contented with one or two *aḥādīth* only in every chapter. He wrote to the scholars of Makka explaining this:

"ولم أكتب فى الباب الا حديثا أو حديثين ، وان كان فى الباب أحاديث صحاح فانه يكثر ، وانما اردت قرب منفعته"

> I do not record more than one or two *aḥādīth* in every chapter though there were other authentic *aḥādīth* concerning the same chapter, as it would be يكثر too much as I meant one which could be used easily.[25]

---

24. Ibn Khair, *Fihrist,* 110. *A'lām an-Nubūwāt* may be the same as *Dalā'il an-Nubūwāt.*
25. Abū Dāwud, His letters to Meccans, p. 23.

He said that even 4 *aḥādīth* out of them are sufficient for a man in this life and the hereafter.

The book was very widely circulated in the author's life itself. 'Alī b. Ḥasan said that he learnt this book six times from Abū Dāwūd. The book is one of the best and more comprehensive than others on the subject of legal *aḥādīth*.

It ought to be remembered that not all the *aḥādīth* recorded by Abū Dāwūd in this book are authentic. Abu Dāwud himself pointed out many weak *aḥādīth,* and there are *aḥādīth* not mentioned by him as weak but the scholars counted them as weak. Why did Abu Dāwud record some weak *ahādīth* in his book *Sunan*?

In the opinion of Abu Dāwud a weak *ḥadīth*—if it were not very weak, just like some student had 50% of the mark—is better than the personal opinion of the scholars. Therefore he recorded them instead of the legal opinions of the early scholars.

Commentaries on *Sunan* of Abū Dawūd

Many commentaries have been written on the book, and the best one available is that Shamsul Haq 'Azīmābādī's, *'Awn al-Ma'būd Sharh Sunan Abi Dāwūd.* An equally good commentary on *Sunan* is *Badh al-Majhūd* Fi Hall Abī Dāwūd by Khalīl Ahmad Ansārī (d.1346). Another very important work has been published under the title *Tahdhīb Sunan Abī Dāwūd* edited by Ahmad Shākir and others in 8 volumes in Cairo, 1367-69/1948-50. It contains the books of Mundhirī and Ibn al-Qayyim, both leading scholars of seventh and eight century of *hijra*. Lately a very valuable study of Abū Dāwūd and his works has been published by a famous scholar Muḥammad Sabbāg.

Many books on *Sunan* basis have been compiled. Here is a small list of those books. We will discuss some of them in detail.

Sunan of Abū Dāwud
Sunan of Tirmidhī
Sunan of Nasa'ī: Kubra and Mujataba
Sunan of Ibn Māja
Sunan of Aḥmad b. 'Ubaid
Sunan of Ismā'īl al-Qāḍī
Sunan of Baihaqī
Sunan of Ibn Juraij

Sunan of Khallāl
Sunan of Dāraquṭnī
Sunan of Dārimī
Sunan of Sa'īd b. Manṣūr
Sunan of Sahl b. Abū Sahl
Sunan of Shāfi'ī
Sunan of Mūsā b. Ṭāriq

8. Muḥammad b. 'Isa b. Saura b. Mūsā b. al-Dahhak at-Tirmidhī

He was born in the year 209 A.H. He began *riḥla* for the study of *ḥadīth* most probably in 235 A.H. and returned to his home town Khurāsān before 250 A.H. He compiled his work after this date. He was very much influenced by Bukhārī, as in his book *'Ilal'* he explicitly states that he did not find one like Bukhārī in Iraq or Khurāsān.

Tirmidhī died on 13th Rajab 279 A.H.

His Works

Al-Jāmi' Al-Mukhtaṣar min as-Sunan 'an Rasulliah.

Tawārikh

al-'Ilal

al-'Ilal al-Kabīr

Shamā' il

Asmā' as-Ṣaḥāba

Al-Asmā' wal-Kūnā

Āl-'Āthār al-Mauqūfa

His most famous work is *Al-Jāmi' or as-Sunan at-Tirmidhī.*

Aims of the Author

a. To collect the *aḥādīth* of the Prophet systematically.

b. To discuss the legal opinions of early Imāms regarding the subject. Therefore he mentioned only those *aḥādīth* which were mentioned by the early scholars as the basis for their legal decisions. However, there are a few *aḥādīth,* may be three or four, which are exempted from this rule.

c. To discuss the quality of *ahādīth* and if there was any *'illa,* weakness or sickness, he would explain it. The book has been divided in 50 sub-books (*kitāb*). It contains altogether 3956 *aḥādīth.*[2]

Nature of the Book *al-Jāmi'* in *Ḥadīth* Collection

A book containing all kinds of *aḥādīth,* is called *Jāmi',* that is, it contains *aḥādīth* concerning *Sīyar* (International law) *Adab* (social behaviour) *Tafsīr* (exegesis of the Qur'ān), *'Aqīda* (belief) *Fitan, Ahkām* (Laws of all kinds) *Al-Ashrāṭ* and *Manāqib* (Biographies of the Prophet and certain companions. As the Sunan of Tirmidhī contains all these chapters, therefore it is named, *Jāmi'* as well. This book was compiled on 10 Dhul-Hijja 270 A.H.

His Method in Arranging His Materials

Tirmidhī puts the heading, then mentions mostly one or two *aḥādīth* from which the heading can be extracted. Afterwards he gives his opinions about the quality of *ḥadīth,* whether it is authentic or good or weak. For this purpose he uses a terminology not used by early scholars. He also mentions the opinions of early Jurists, Lawyers and Imāms concerning the subject. More than this, he also indicates if there were *aḥādīth* transmitted by the other Companions concerning the same subject, even if it has its connection in a wider range.

Commentaries on the *Sunan* of Tirmidhī

There have been many commentaries compiled on this work. The best one available at present is the work of 'Abdur Rahmān Mubārakpurī, titled: *Tuhfat al-Aḥwadhī* in 4 volumes and has been reprinted several times.

9. Abū 'Abdullah Muḥammad b. Yazīd ar-Rab'ī (Ibn Majah)

Known as Ibn Mājah al-Qazwīnī.

He was born in 209 A.H.

It is not mentioned at what age he began the study of *ḥadīth*. 'Alī b. Muḥammad al-Tanāfasī (d.233) was the earliest of his teachers. It means that Ibn Mājah began the study of *ḥadīth* before 233 A.H. at about 15 or 20 as it was the custom of that period. He began his journey for the learning of *ḥadīth* after 230 A.H. He visited Khurasan, Iraq, Ḥijāz, Syria, Egypt etc. He died on Monday, 21 of Ramdān, 273 A.H. His son 'Abdullah has been mentioned as the one who put him in the grave, and was assisted by his two uncles. The scholars are unanimous on Ibn Majah's great scholarship and trustworthiness.

His Works

Tafsīr.

Al-Tārīkh, (biography of the narrator of *aḥādīth*)

Sunan

At present we have no information about his *Tafsīr* and *Tārīkh*. It seems that both of them have been lost for a long time. However, *Sunan* of Ibn Māja is very famous. Hundreds of libraries contain manuscripts of this work. This book has been published many times. In a later period it became one of the six famous books which are called الأصول الستة Six principal works or sometimes الصحاح الستة 'the Six authentic books.' It does not mean that all the *aḥādīth* recorded in these six books are authentic, it means that majority of them are authentic, with exception of the *Ṣaḥīḥ* of Bukhārī and that of Muslim in which all are.

His Methodology for Selecting the Material

He did not mention his criteria for selecting the materials. Neither did he mention the aim he had in his mind in compiling this work. His book is of the lowest grade in the collection of the Six Principal works. His books contain 4341 *aḥādīth,* out of them 3002 have been recorded by authors of the remaining five books, either by all or by one of them. There remain 1339 *aḥādīth* which have been recorded by Ibn Māja alone and not recorded by the other five. These may be put in the following gradings:

428 *aḥādīth* out of 1339 are authentic.

199 *aḥādīth* out of 1339 are good.

613 *aḥādīth* out of 1330 are of weak *isnād.*

99 *aḥādīth* out of 1339 are of *munkar* or *makdhub.*[26]

The other scholars, such as Abū Dāwūd and Tirmidhī also recorded weak *aḥādīth,* but they mostly noted them in their book, but Ibn Maja, even when he recorded a false *ḥadīth,* went on silently. Therefore a lot of discussion has gone on among scholars about this book to the effect that some other books deserve to be mentioned in Six Principle works instead of that by Ibn Māja. Scholars like Ibn al-Athīr (d.606) Mughlatā'ī (d. 762), Ibn Hajar (d.852) and Questallānī (d.923), disliked putting this book with the other five books. As a matter of fact, to count it as one of the six principle works or to take it out of them would not affect the book by any way. Because, every *ḥadīth* recorded in these books is searched according to its own merit and not as a *ḥadīth* quoted from one of the six works.

How it Became One of the Six Books

There is nothing reported from the early scholars that there are or there ought to be six principle works. It came accidentally due to literary process. In the third and the fourth century hundreds of books were compiled. Some of them became more famous than others. Therefore scholars began to write books on the biographies of the narrators whose *aḥādīth* have been recorded in certain book, so that other scholars may easily judge the value of every *ḥadīth.*

For example Ibn 'Adī (d.365), Dāraqutnī (d.385) al-Kalābādhī (d.398) and many other scholars compiled works on the narrators who have been mentioned by Bukhārī in his *Ṣaḥīḥ.* This is not only with Bukhārī but the same happened with other works such as books of Muslim, Abū Dāwūd etc.

In later periods, scholars began to combine two or more books, such as the combination of the materials of Bukhārī and Muslim by Humaidī, Saghānī etc. On the same pattern some scholars began to combine the two works written on the biographies of Bukhārī and Muslim.

26. F-'Abdul Bāqi note on *Sunan* Ibn Māja, pp. 1519-20.

However, 'Abdul Ghanī b. 'Abdul Wāḥid al-Maqdisī (d. 600) compiled a work called *Al-Kamāl* in which he collected all the narrators who have been mentioned in any of the Six books, namely, Sahīh of Bukhārī, Sahīh of Muslim, *Sunan* of Nasa'i, *Sunan* of Abū Dāwūd, *Sunan* of Tirmidhī, and *Sunan* of Ibn Māja. This work became the base for many famous works on the dictionary of the narrators, such as Mizzī, Dhahabī, Ibn Kathīr, Mughlatā'ī, Khazrajī and Ibn Ḥajar etc.

Thus the reckoning of Ibn Maja as one of the six principal books is due to Maqdisī's work. Later on scholars began to mention these six works together. As their narrators were mentioned in a single book, these six books began to appear as a single unit. But to put any book in this single unit or to take it out does not add to, or detract from, the value of the book or material in it, because, as I have mentioned earlier, every single *ḥadīth* is tested according to its own merit and not by the prestige of its recorder.

Main Feature of *Sunan* of Ibn Maja.

The book has very little repetition, and it is one of the best in arrangement of chapters and sub-chapters, a fact which is recognized by many scholars. It is divided–in the edition of M. Fuwād 'Abdul Bāqī–in 37 chapters (*kitāb*) and contains 4341 *aḥādīth*.

Commentaries of *Sunan* of Ibn Maja

It has not been very lucky in attracting the attention of scholars. Very few commentaries have been written. The best one perhaps–is of Mughlatā'ī (d.762) titled: *Al-I'lām bi Sunanihi 'Alaihis-Salām* (incomplete) and not published yet.

10. Abul Qāsim Sulaimān b. Aḥmad b. Ayyūb al-Ṭabarānī al-Lakhamī

His family belonged to Yemeni tribe Lakhm who migrated to Quds and settled down there. His mother belonged to 'Akka. He was born in 'Akka in the month of *Ṣafar* 260 A.H. It seems that his father was very fond of education, so he directed his son for the learning of *ḥadīth* in very early age. He began the study of *ḥadīth* in early age. Dhahabi mentioned that Tabarānī began to learn *aḥādīth* in 273 A.H. in Ṭabarīya. It means that he was at that time about 13 years old. In 274 A.H. he went to Quds for the study. In 275 A.H. he was in Qaisariya for the same purpose. He made extensive journeys for this purpose and visited Syria, Egypt, Yeman, Arabian Peninsula, the Present Iran Afghanistan etc. He spent some 30 years in the learning of *ḥadīth* and the number of his teachers exceeds one thousand. He visited Aṣfahān for the sake of study in 290 A.H. After finishing his study in that city he went to other places, but he returned back to Aṣfahān and chose it as his home and lived there for more than half a century. Ṭabarānī died in 360 A.H.

It seems that the Governor of Asfahān Ibn Rustum fixed for him certain amounts and he used to receive it. He is one of those scholars who compiled very large number of books.

Here is an incomplete list of his works. Most of his books perished in early days. Sezgin mentions some 13 works under his name, even not all of them belong to Ṭabarānī. Thus about 10 of his works are known to us at present.

He has not been so lucky in attracting the attention of modern scholars. Only one of his books *al-Mu'jam aṣ-Ṣaghīr* has been published and that too is full of mistakes.

His Works

Musnad al-'Ashara
Musnad ash-Shāmiyīn
An-Nawādir
Fawā'id.

Musnad Abū Huraira
Musnad 'Ā'isha.
Tafsīr al-Qur'ān
Du'ā'
Dalā'il an-Nubūwa.
Aḥādīth at-Ṭiwāl
Hadīth Shu'ba
Hadīth A'mash
Ḥadīth Auzā'ī
Ḥadīth Shaibān
Ḥadīth Ayyūb.
'Ishrat an-Nisā'
Musnad Abū Dharr
Ar-Ru'yā'
Al-Jūd.
Faḍl Ramadān
Al-Farā'd
Ar-Radd'alā al-Mu'tazila
Aṣ-Ṣalāt 'ala ar-Rasul
Aḥādīth Zuhrī from Anas
Aḥādīth Ibn al-Munkadir from Jābir
Ḥadīth man Kadhab.
Akhbār 'Umar b. 'Abdul-'Azīz etc.
Al-Mu'Jam as Ṣaghīr

But his most famous work is *Al-Mu'jam al-Kabīr* in 12 volumes.

This is the Encyclopaedia of *hadīth* which contains not only *ahādīth* of the Prophet but a great deal of historical information as well. This book has absorbed totally or partially hundreds of early works. The work ought to be published after critical edition. Several libraries contain different volumes of this work, but at present it is difficult to say that it would complete the work or not. The second work which was very dear to Tabārānī is his *al-Mu'jam al-Awsat,* in which he collected mostly rare information and knowledge concerning *ahādīth,* some of the authentic and other non-authentic.

Al-Hamdulillah it is complete in two huge volumes in Istanbul and needs editing and publishing.

The smallest one in this series is his *al-Mu'jam as-Saghīr* which has been published twice. The second edition is the worst one. In this book he recorded one *ḥadīth* on the authority of each of his teachers. Thus the numbers of his teachers exceeds thousands.

He died in Aṣfahān on 28th Dhīqa'da 360, at the age of one hundred years and ten months.

Nature of *Mu'jam* Work

It differs from one author to another one. Sometimes it is arranged according to alphabetical names of the Companions other times according to regions and some other times according to the alphabetical names of the teachers of compilers as has been done by Ṭabarānī in his *Mu'jam aṣ-ṣaghīr.*

Here is a list of some famous Mu'jams:

Mu'jam Ṣafar by Silafī
Mu'jam Ṣafar by Sammān
Mu'jam by Isma'īlī
Mu'jam by Ibn al-A'rabī
Mu'jam by Ibn Shāhīn
Mu'jam al-Kabīr by Dhahabi
Mu'jam Niswān by Ibn 'Asākir
Mu'jam Shuyukh by Ḥakim
Mu'jam Shuyukh by Dimyātī
Mu'jam Shuyukh by Ibn al-Muqrī

11. Abu as-Sa'ādāt al-Mubārak b. Muḥammad b. 'Abdul Karīm al-Jazarī (Ibn al-Athīr al-Jazarī)

He belongs to a famous literary family. They were three brothers. Mubārak b. Muḥammad, a *Muḥaddith,* 'Ali b. Muḥammed, a historian, author of *al-Kāmil Fit-Tārikh,* Naṣrullah b. Muḥammad, a man of literature, and author of many literary works. It is very surprising that all of them are known by the name of Ibn al-Athīr.

He was born in 554 A.H. in Jazīrah of Ibn 'Umar, a town north of Mausil. In 565 A.H. he came to Mausil and made it his permanent residence.

Ibn al-Athir was a very religious man, and a scholar of very high rank. He was the leading figure in Arabic language, exegesis of the Qur'ān, Grammar, liguistics, *hadīth* and *Fiqh* (Islamic law).

He continuously held important advisory posts in government. Several governors and even the Government changed, but all of the rulers were in need of him. He was offered a ministerial post but refused it. His refusal caused some anger to the authorities, but he explained his stand and satisfied them.

His Works

He compiled many works in different fields of knowledge. Here is a list of few of them.

An-Nihāyah fī Gahrīb al-Ḥadīth.
Ash-Shāfī fī sharh musnad ash-shāfi'ī
Al-Inṣāf bainal-Kashf wa al-Kashshaf.
Jāmi' al-Usūl Fī Aḥādīth ar-Rasūl

In later days he suffered from gout (joint pain) in his leg and was unable to stretch his leg or walk.

The King and ministers used to visit him asking for his experience and sincere advices. Later on a physician came from Maghrib and treated with some ointment. There was good improvement but Ibn Al-Athīr asked his brother to pay the physician and discharge him. The brother was astonished and asked him why he was taking such a decision while there is a good improvement. He replied: Well, you are right, but now I am in comfort from the authorities. I dislike to go to their doors, and prefer to live in peace and comfort. When I was healthy I used to go to their doors, now they come to me in important matters. Therefore rest of the life I want to spend in freedom from those people. His brother followed his advice, and Ibn al-Athīr was contented to live with the severe pain.

It is said that all his literary works are productions of his days of illness. He used to dictate to his students and by this way his books were compiled.

He died in 606 A.H. in Mausil.

Main Features of *Jamiʿ al-Uṣūl*

He collected all the *aḥādīth* of the Prophet recorded in:
Muwatta' of Imām Mālik,
Ṣaḥīḥ of Bukhārī
Ṣaḥīḥ of Muslim
Jāmiʿ of Tirmidhī
Sunan of Nasa'ī
Sunan of Abū Dāwūd.

First of all he omitted all the *asānīd.* Afterwards he arranged the chapters according to alphabetic order. For example in *Sunan* work, first chapter begins with *Ṭahāra* (cleansing) but the letter T comes in the sixteen number. Thus his book began with Imān and Islam الإيمان والإسلام which are written in Arabic by the first letter A. When he records a *ḥadīth* he mentions that out of those six authors who recorded it in their books. He mostly keeps the wordings of Bukhārī and Muslim, and describes if there were variants in expression. Then he gives the meanings of the difficult words. However, when consulting this book and quoting from it, one should not refer to original works such as Bukhārī to give expression that this original work was consulted. In case one wants to be sure of exact words of the authority mentioned, one must go to the original work.

However, the book is very useful to scholars. It has been published more than once, and the best edition until now is the edition of ʿAbdul Qādir al-Arnāwūt of Damascus.

12. 'Alī b. Abū Bakr b. Sulaimān al-Haithamī

He was born in Rajab 735 A.H. He studied the Qur'ān and after reaching the age of maturity, he joined the famous *ḥadīth* scholar of his time Zainuddīn al'Irāqī. He accompanied Zainuddīn in most of his journeys for *Ḥajj* or for learning of *hadīth*. Thus Zainuddīn was his teacher as well as his colleague, because both of them studied together under many famous scholars.

Zainuddīn gave al-Haithamī his daughter in marriage. Moreover, he taught Haithamī the science of *ḥadīth*. Under his buidance Haithamī learned the method of extracting *Zawā'id,* that is to select only those *aḥādīth* which are not mentioned by some particular scholars. Haithamī was a great expert on this subject. He compiled many works on Zāwa'id, that is he collected only those *aḥādīth* which were in the said book but were not found in the Six Principal books.

He compiled *Zawā'id* of *Musnad Aḥmad* on Six principal works and named it *Ghāyatul Maqṣad Fi Zawā'id Ahmad,* and *Musnad of al-vazzār* and named it *Al-Baḥr az-zakhkhār Fī Zawā'id al-Bazzār,* and that of *Musnad of Abū Ya'lā,* and that of *al-Mu'jam al-Kabīr* of Tabarānī and named it *Al-Badir al-Munīr Fi Zawā'id al-Mu'jam al-Kabīr* and that of *al-Mu'jam aṣ-Ṣaghīr* and *al-Awṣat* and named it *Majma' al-Bahrain Fī Zawā'id al-Mu'jamaīn.*

Besides these he compiled many other works on the same pattern. However, he collected all those above mentioned works in one single work named *Majima' az-Zawā'id wa manba' al-Fawā'id.* He dropped the *isnād* totally, arranged the book according to *Jāmi'* and *Sunan* pattern, explaining the grade of *ḥadīth* or mentioning names of narrators who were impugned, though his gradings were not always acceptable to later scholars. The book was published in 10 volumes by Qudsī in Cairo in 1352 A.H.

The author stripped *aḥādīth* from *isnād* for the sake of brevity, but it created a sort of defect in the work. However, it is a great Encyclopaedia of *ḥadīth*. Haithamī was praised very much by his contemporaries and later scholars. He died on 19th Ramadān 807 A.H.

13. Jalāluddīn 'Abdur Raḥmān b. Kamāluddīn As-Suyutī

He was born on 1st Rajab 849 A.H. His father died while he was only six years old. He was reared in the guardianship of Ash-Shihāb b. At-Ṭabbākh. However, he had very good opportunity for learning. In the list of his teachers we find almost all the famous scholars of his time and their number reaches up to 150 scholars.

The number of works compiled by him is about six hundred, some of them in a page or two while some others in many volumes. His main activity was to abridge the books of early scholars. By this he gained the enmity of many scholars who accused him of stealing the materials of early scholars.

He was Principal of many academic institutions. Due to certain conspiracies and jealousies he was relieved of the post. Later on, when the same post was offered to him he refused to accept it. He was very much respected and high ranking officials used to visit him.

His Works

As I mentioned earlier his works are in great numbers reaching up to 600. The one which concerns us here is his comprehensive collection of *aḥādīth* of the Prophet.

We have seen earlier that Ibn al-Athīr and Haithamī collected *aḥādīth* from several books and arranged them into one book.

However Ibn Ḥajar (d.852) thought of collecting all the *aḥādīth* of the Prophet in a single book but he abandoned this idea. Later on his pupil Suyūtī thought on the same line and compiled the following works:

Al-Jāmi' al-Kabir or Jam'ul-Jawāmi'

Suyūtī intended to collect all the *aḥādīth* of the Prophet in a single book.

He divided the work in two sections:

a) Sayings of the Prophet.

b) Actions of the Prophet.

Into the first section, he arranged alphabetically the sayings of the Prophet.

However in second section concerning actions, he arranged them according to the Companions separately. He omitted the *isnād* totally and referred to the authorities who endorsed the particular *ḥadīth* in his book.

He provided a lengthy list of the works on *ḥadīth,* whose material he had collected already. He mentioned the list so that in the event of his death any other scholar could continue the work.

However, he died without its completion. During this period, he made two small collections mostly from the material of his *Al-Jāmi' al-Kabīr* "the Grand Collection." These are:

1. *Al-Jāmi' aṣ-Ṣaghīr* which contains 10010 *aḥādīth.* There are the sayings of the Prophet arranged in alphabetical order without *isnād.* He completed this work on 907 A.H.
2. *Ziyādāt 'ala al-jāmi' aṣ-Ṣaghīr.*
   After finishing *al-Jāmi' as-Saghīr,* he collected quite good quantity of material and arranged them in the pattern of *Jāmi' Saghīr* and made it the supplement. However Yusuf an-Nabahānī mixed the material of these books together in one unit on the pattern of Suyūtī and named it *Al-Fatḥul Kabīr Fi Dammaz-Ziyādāt ila al-Jāmi' aṣ-Ṣaghīr.* It was published in 3 volumes in Egypt in 1351/1932. As the original work was arranged in alphabetical order and not according to subject, therefore it was very difficult to use these books.

An Indian Scholar 'Alī b. Ḥisāmuddin (d.975 in Makka) known as Al-Muttaqī al-Hindī arranged all the material of these three books according to legal chapter and named it *Kanzul 'Ummāl Fī Sunan al-Aqwāl wal-Af'āl.* This is the greatest collection of *aḥādīth* in a single book. The book has been published twice in Hyderbad in India.

As the collection contains all sorts of ahadīth and Suyūtī's judgments on the authenticity of *ḥadīth* is not sound, therefore the book is not useful for general reading. However, there is a need for a comprehensive collection. I pray Allah to give me courage to fulfill this duty.

Suyūtī died in 911 A.H. in Cairo.

14. Books on Subjects Related to *Ḥadīth*

I have described only a few books out of many hundreds relating purely to *ḥadīth* literature. However, there are many many topics and problems related to *ḥadīth* and *ḥadīth* literature and many books have been compiled on every related subject. Below I am going to give a list of some subjects on which books are found in *ḥadīth* literature.

Let us begin first with the general conditions of teaching and learning.

1. There are books on the behaviour, etiquette and conditions which ought to be fulfilled by the teacher. One of the best books on the subject is *Al-Jāmi' Li Akhlāq ar-Rāwī wa' ādab as-Sāmi'* by Khaṭīb al-Baghdadi.

2. On the method to be applied by teachers in dictation, there is a good book called *Adab al-Imlā' wa al-Istimlā'* by Sam'ānī.

3. About students and journey for learning of *aḥādīth,* there is a book called *ar-Riḥla* by Khaṭīb.

However, there are many chapters in *al-Jāmi'* (mentioned under No. 1) concerning students.

4. As far as it concerns the question of writing down of *aḥādīth,* there is a good book by Khaṭīb Baghdādī called *Taqyīd al-'Ilm.* A comprehensive study of the subject has been carried out by the present writer, titled: *Studies in Early Ḥadith Literature.*

5. What method should be used for revision and corrections after writing down *aḥādīth,* one of the best books on the subject is *al-Ilmā'* by Qāḍī 'Ayāḍ.

6. To evaluate the certain certificates given to students by teachers, there are books on the subject such as *Al-wajāza Fī Tajwīz al-Ijāza* by Mu'ammarī.[27]

I have described earlier, that *aḥādīth* have been sorted out by different kinds. There are books containing only one sort of *aḥādīth,* such as:

---

27. *Tabrīb* II, 52.

7. Books containing *Mutawātir aḥādīth*[28] such as: *Al-Azhār al-Mutanathira* by Suyūtī.

8. Books containing *aḥādīth Qudsī*[29] such as: *Al-Itḥāfāt as-Sanīya* by Manāwī.

9. Books containing *aḥādīth* which had *'Illa,* some hidden defect such as: *Al'Ilal* by Dāraquṭnī.

10. Some orders of the Prophet were abrogated by him in later period. There are books containing this sort of *aḥādīth,* such as *Al-I'tibār Fi an-Nāsikh wa al-Mansūkh min al-'Āthar* by Ḥāzimi.

11. Certain sayings of the Prophet had relation with certain occasion, to describe these occasions there are books such as: *Asbāb warūd al-Aḥādīth* by Husainī.

12. Sometimes one finds two *aḥādīth* seemingly contradictory, to clear their meanings and to reconcile them, there are books such as *Ikhtilāf al-Ḥadīth* by *Shāfi'ī, and Tā'wīl Mukhtalaf al-Ḥadīth* by Ibn. Qutaibah.

13. Every subject has its own dictionary. We find legal dictionaries, technical dictionaries etc. Likewise there are dictionaries relating to *aḥādīth.* There are many dictionaries of this sort, one of them commonly used by Scholars is *Nihāya* by Ibn al-Athīr in four volumes.

14. When it comes to commentaries, there are hundreds of books of commentaries on *ḥadīth.* Sezgin has referred to 56 commentaries on *Ṣaḥīḥ* of Bukhārī only. If we collect it with other books which deal with *Ṣaḥīḥ* of Bukhārī by one way or other, it would exceed one hundred.

Even pure *ḥadīth* literature has been divided in many subdivisions according to the methods applied by compilers in arranging the material. I have discussed earlier the books called (1) *Musnad,* (2), *Ṣaḥīḥ,* (3) *Jami',* (4) *Sunan,* (5) *Mu'Jam,* and (6) *Zawā'id.*

However, there are many other divisions such as *Mustakhraj, Juz', Fawāid, Mashā'ikh. Mustakhraj,* that is a later scholar chooses one of the early works like *Ṣaḥīḥ* of Bukhārī, and narrates the same *ḥadīth* in his book passing Bukhārī, joining *isnād* of Bukhārī in upper part mostly with the teacher of Bukhārī. There are many books written on this pattern by later scholars.

---

28. For definition see above p. 43
29. For definition see above p. 44

Juz'

This sort of book contains either a good collection of *aḥādīth* on a single topic as *Juz' al-Qirā't* by Bukhārī, or they collect narration of a single narrator in one book like *Juz'* of Ibn 'Arafa etc. It exceeds a few thousand.[30]

Mauḍu'at

On spurious *aḥādīth* there are many books, for example by Ibn al-Jauzī Suyuṭī, Mulla 'Ali Qārī and Shaukānī. The work of Mullā 'Alī Qārī *Mauḍū 'āt Kabīr* and of Shaukānī, *al-Fawā'id al-Majmu'a* are very useful for general readers.

No doubt there were no facilities of modern printing and thus it was not possible to make indexing system as it is used now. But *Muḥaddithīn* developed from the first century a method for learning called *Atrāf*, that is to refer only to beginning of *hadīth*. Basing on this system many books were compiled which were used as indexing of *ḥadīth*. One of the best ones which is still in print is entitled *Tuḥfatul Ashrāf* by Mizzī.

When it comes to the biographies of the narrators, it may be divided into several categories.

a. Histories of a particular city. It was the fashion of the Muslim scholars that they used to write the history of the cities, which were actually the biographies of the famous scholars of the city. It need not be mentioned that reference to *Muḥaddithīn* in these histories has the lion's share. We may say in few early centuries, every city in Muslim world had not one history, but several, with many supplements. For example History of Baghdād by Khaṭīb (d. 463) which has been published in 14 volumes has several supplements such as supplement of Sam'ānī in 15 volumes, of Dubaithī in 3 volumes, of Najjār in 30 volumes.

History of Damascus by Ibn 'Asākir (d.571) in 80 volumes. Even this grand history has many supplements. Second method for compiling biographies was to compile a book on the narrators mentioned in certain books. For example biographies of the narrators whose name occurs in the book of *Sahīh* of Bukhārī, by Ibn Abu 'Adī, (d.365) *Daraqutnī* (d.385), Kalābādhī (d.398), al-Bājī (d.474) etc. This is not confined to *Sahīh* of Bukhārī only but most of the famous books on *ahādīth* had this sort of books.

The third method for compiling the biographies of narrators was to mention only one type of narrators such as trustworthy, (*thiqāt*) such as

30. Kattānī, *Risala Mustarafa* 94.

Thiqat by Ibn Hibbān, 'Ijlī, Ibn Shāhin etc. Or book on *weak* narrators. Even the weakness comes by different causes. For example: weakness due to failure of memory in old age. I may mention in this regard *Kashf al-Iltibās bi man rumiya bil-Ikhtilāṭ* by Ibn al-'Ajamī or a sort of weakness because the narrator used to practice *Tadlis,* in this regard one of the best books is *Jāmi' at-Taḥṣīl* by al-'Alā'ī, etc.

However there are other books which deal with the weak narrators in general. The most famous one is *al-Kāmil* by Ibn 'Adī, (d.365) still unpublished. One of the best books published on weak narrators is that of Dhahabi, called *Mizān al-I'tidāl.*

The fourth method for compiling the biographies of narrators was to mention the narrators irrespective of their weakness or trustworthiness or whether they lived in this city or that or whether their *aḥādīth* were found in one book or another. One may mention in this regard *Tārīkh* of Ibn Ma'īn of Al-Fasawī, of Ibn Abū Khaithama, of Ibn Abū Ḥātim ar-Rāzī and *at Tārīkh al-Kabīr* of Bukhārī. The later two books have been published in Hyderabad.

As the Companions of the Prophet had special reverence among the narrators, many books have been written on their biographies. One of the best ones is *Al-Isāba Fī Tamyīz aṣ-Ṣahāba* by Ibn Ḥajar. Sometimes men become famous through their nicknames, الالقاب. There are dictionaries of the people famous by nicknames exceeding fifty volumes[31] called *Majm'ul al-Alqāb* by Ibn al-Fūtī.

Sometimes men are known by *Kunya* 'surname' like Abu al-Qāsim, Abū Ahmad, meaning father of Aḥmad. In Arab tradition, this is one of the means of respect, instead of naming him directly one might call the man father of so and so. There are many books written on *Kunā,* because very frequently a narrator in *Isnād* was mentioned by surname or *Kunya.*

For early narrators one of the best ones is *Al-Kunā* by Dulābī (d.310), and the book has been published in two volumes in Hyderābād, India.

There are so many other subjects and so many books that it needs a separate book on the subject. However, those who can read Arabic, may consult *ar-Risāla al-Mustaṭrafa* by Kattānī, the best book available on the bibliography dealing with the subject of *ḥadīth* and related materials.

31. Ziriklī, *A'lām* IV, 124.

Bibliography

Abū 'Awāna, *Al-Musnad* 1st edition, Hydrābād, India.

Abū Dāwūd, *Sunan,* 4 vols. edited by M. M. 'Abdul Ḥamīd 2nd. emp. Cairo, 1369/1950. *His letters to Maccan,* ed. by M. *Sabbāgh,* Beirut 1395.

Abū Nu'aim, Aḥmad b. 'Abdullah al-Iṣbahānī, *Ḥilyat al-Awliyā',* Khanjī, Cairo, 1932

Abū 'Ubaid Al-Qāsim b. Sallām, *Al-Amwāh,* ed. by M. al-Fiqī, Cairo, 1353

Azami, M. M. a—*Introduction to Kitāb al Tamyīz,* see Muslim, *Tamyīz;*
b—*Kuttāb an-Nabī,* Beirut, 1394;
c—*On Schacht's Origins of Muhammedan Jurisprudence* (under print), University of Riyadh;
d—*Studies in Early Ḥadīth Literature,* Maktab Islami, Beirut, 1968

Al-Balādhurī, Aḥmad b. Yaḥyā, *Ansāb al-Ashrāf,* 1st vol. ed. by Ḥamidulla, Cairo, 1959

Al-Bukhārī, Muḥammad b. Ismā'īl, *Al-Jāmi' as-Sahīh,* printed with *Fatḥul* Bārī. Salafiya Press, Cairo

Dāraquṭnī, *Sunan,* 4 volumes, Cairo

Dhahabī, *Mīzānal-I'tidāl,* 4 vol. ed. by al-Bijāwī, Cairo, 1382/1963

Al-'Ibar ed. by Munajjid, Kuwait

Siyar al-A'lām an-Nubalā'; 1-3 vols. ed. by Munajjid and other, Cairo, 1956

Dārimī, 'Abdullah b. 'Abdur Raḥmān, *Sunan,* 2 vols. edited by M. A. Dahmān, Damascus, 1349

Al-Haithamī, 'Alī b. Abū Bakr, *Majma' az-Zawā'id,* 10 vols., Qudsi, Cairo, 1352

Hājī Khalīfa, Musatfa b. 'Abdulla, *Kashf al-Zunūn 'an Asāmī al-Kutub wa al-Funun,* Calcutta, 1865

Al-Hākim, Muhammad b. 'Abdulla, a—*Al-Madkhal,* ed. and translated by J. Robson Luzack, London, 1953; b—*Al-Mustadrak,* 4 volumes, Hydrabad

Ḥamīdullah, *al-Wathā'iq al-Siyāsiya,* 3rd ed., Beirut, 1968

Ibn Abu Hatim al-Rāzī, 'Abdur Raḥmān, *Al-Jarḥ Wa al-Ta'dīl* with introduction, 9 volumes, Hydrabad, 1360-1373

Ibn Ḥajar, a—*Fatḥul Bārī,* ed by M. Fuwād, 'Abdul Bāqī, Cairo, 1380; b—*Hadyal-Sārī,* 2 vols., Cairo, 1383; c—*Al-Iṣāba fi Tamyīz aṣ-Ṣaḥāba,* 4 vols., Cairo, 1358

Ibn Hanbal, *Musnad,* 6 vols., Cairo, 1313

Ibn Ḥibbān, Muḥammad b. Ḥibbān al-Bustī, *Ṣaḥīḥ ibn Ḥibbān,* 1st vol. ed., Cairo, 1952; *Majrūḥīn min al-Muḥaddithīn,* Aya Sofya Ms. No. 496 Istanbul

Ibn Isḥāq, *Sīrat Rasulillāh,* translated by A. Guillaume, Oxford Univ. Press, Karachi

Ibn Kathir Ismā'īl, *Tafsīr,* 7 vols., Beirut, 1968

Ibn Khair, Muḥammad b. Khair, *Fihrist,* Baghdad, 1963

Ibn Mājā, *Muḥammad b. Yazīd,* Sunan 2 vols. ed. by M. F. A. Bāqī, Cairo, 1373

Ibn Rāhwaih, Isḥāq b. Rāhwaih, *Musnad,* Egyptian Library, Ms. No. 776, Cairo

Ibn Rajab, 'Abdur Raḥmān b. Aḥmad al-Ḥanbalī, *Sharḥ 'Ilal al-Tirmidhī,* Ẓāhiriya Lib. Ms. Damascus

Ibn Sa'd, Muḥammad b. Sa'd, *Al-Ṭabaqāt al-Kabīr,* 9 vols. ed. by E. Sachan, Leiden 1904-1940

Jurjānī, Al-Sharīf 'Alī, *Risāla fi fann Uṣūl al-Ḥadīth.* Printed with *Jami'* Tirmidhī, Delhi, no date.

Al-Jazā' irī, *Tawjīh an-Naẓar.*

Al-Kattānī, Muḥammad b. Ja'far *Al-Risāla al-Mustatrafa,* 3rd ed. Damascus, 1964

Al-Khaṭīb al-Baghdādī, Ahmad b. 'Alī, a—*al-Kifāya fī 'Ilm al-Ḥadīth,* Hydrabad, 1357; b—*Al-Faqīh Wal Mutafaqqih,* printed in Riyadh, 2 volumes; c—*Al-Rihla* ed. by Sāmarrā'ī; d—*Al-Jāmi' fī Akhlāq ar-Rāwī wa 'Ādāb as-Sāmi',* E. Alexandria Municipal Library Ms. Egypt

Lane, E. W., *Arabic English Lexicon,* 8 volumes, Edinburgh, 1867

Mālik b. Anas, *Muwaṭṭa',* 2 vols. ed. by M. F. 'Abdul Bāqī, Cairo, 1370

Muslim b. Hajjāj al-Qushairī, a—*Ṣaḥiḥ,* ed. by M. F. 'Abdul Bāqī, Cairo, 1374; b—*Tamyīz,* ed. by M. M. Azami, Univ. of Riyadh, 1395

Mu'allimī al-Yamānī, 'Abdur Raḥmān b. Yaḥyā, *Al-Anwār al-Kāshifa,* Cairo, 1378; *Al-Tankīl,* 2 vols., ed. by Nāṣiruddīn Al-Albānī.

Nāsiruddīn, Asad, *Musādir ash-Shi'r al Jāhilī,* 2nd ed. Darul Ma'ārif, Cairo, 1962

Penrice, John, *Dictionary and the Glossary of the Koran,* London, 1873

D. Auvray, *Introduction A La Bible,* Paris

The Holy *Qur'ān:* The Words of Allah

Suyutī, 'Abdur Raḥmān b. Abu Bakr

Tadrīb ar-Rāwī, ed. by A. R. Latīf, Cairo, 1379

Al-Durril-Manthūr, 6 vols., Cairo.

Tirmidhī, Muḥammad b. 'Isā, *Sunan,* ed. by Shākir and others, 5 vols., Cairo

Al-Zurqānī, Muhammad b. 'Abdul Bāqī, *Sharḥ Muwaṭṭa',* 4 vols., Cairo

Zafar Ansāri, *Islamic Juristic Terminology.*

www.ingramcontent.com/pod-product-compliance
Lightning Source LLC
Chambersburg PA
CBHW051834040426
42447CB00006B/521
* 9 7 8 0 8 9 2 5 9 0 1 1 7 *